WARM MEMORIES OF COLD SPRING

Snapshots

of a

Mid-Twentieth Century

Love Story

Beatrice Fulton Keeber

Text and art © 2013 Beatrice Fulton Keeber

All Rights Reserved.

COVER ILLUSTRATION AND INSIDE ILLUSTRATIONS BY TONY DE LUZ

TABLE OF CONTENTS

AUTHOR'S NOTE 1

THE WAR'S OVER, NOW GO CELEBRATE! 3

VALENTINE'S DAY, 1946 7

FIRST DATE 11

SODA FOUNTAIN 16

STUDENT UNION LUNCHES 21

THE VETS' WELCOME DANCE 25

DANCING AT HOME 27

CHESTNUT LODGE 32

OUR FIRST NEW DATE – OF MANY MORE 40

THE COURSE OF TRUE LOVE NEVER RUNS SMOOTHLY.......... 45

THE SURPRISING BIRTHDAY GIFT 51

A NEW DATE DRESS 54

THE NOT-QUITE-PROPOSAL 58

THE GREEN-EYED MONSTER 61

I FOUND US AN APARTMENT! 67

THE FORGOTTEN WEDDING 70

HONEYMOON DAZED 76

COLD SPRING 78

HONKY-TONK HYMNS	80
HOME, SWEET HOME	83
WILLARD, WILLARD! RUN QUICK!	89
THE FUNERAL	95
LAUNDRY LESSONS	100
CULINARY ARTS 101	103
GAIL ELIZABETH — and a couple of other issues	109
HAPPY NEW YEAR, SWEETHEART (1950)	118
THE CHANGELING LANDLADY	121
YOU COULD ALWAYS GO TO MY MOTHER	124
COULD WE REALLY DO THAT?	127
THE DAY THE CEILING FELL	129
BILL'S PLAN	132
THE BANK	134
NUMBER 10 WAVERLEY STREET	138
A MOUSE IN THE PANTRY!	144
DAVID WILLIAM	148
MOTHER CAME TO HELP	152
DORSEY, WAGNER AND CROSBY – FOR BABYSITTERS?	157
THE NEW DISHWASHER	159

HOW ABOUT ANOTHER BABY?	164
JOHN WILLARD	168
THE GRIM REAPER - AGAIN	174
GROCERY EXPEDITIONS	179
NEIGHBORS	183
BETHANIE LORRAINE	200
HOW COULD WE POSSIBLY SPEND THAT MUCH MONEY?	205
OLEY	208
GOODBYE, HOUSE!	212
MOVING ON	217
THE DISASTER HOUSE	222
AND STILL MORE DISASTERS!	226
THE NEW HOUSE	228
ANNE MARGARET	231
THOSE BUSY WESTFIELD YEARS	233
MIDDLESEX	235
DISCIPLINE FOR DUMMIES!	238
SENTIMENTAL JOURNEY HOME	245
— AND THEN WHAT HAPPENED?	249

AUTHOR'S NOTE

Can you *believe* the hat Grandma's wearing in that picture? ... Snapshots and memories are moments frozen in time. The people we see and recall in them were so *different* from us! Or were they? Did they worry about things the way we do? Could they possibly have loved as deeply as we do? Is time travel possible? Could we step into their shoes for just a moment?

This is a snapshot of times past, never to return again — except in their essential similarities to present day lives. The most important lesson I learned from those years is love. Without that, none of this would have been worthwhile. With it, everything was worthwhile.

All recollections in this book are factual, but may have been edited for purposes of clarity or brevity. Dialogue is recalled to the best of my recollection, but — if reported any differently from actual wording — remains true to original intent. Except for my immediate family, names and identifying details may have been altered in the interest of privacy.

I appreciate the help and influence of so many people without whom this book would not have been possible. First, of course, my wonderful late husband, Willard Keeber, the other half of this love affair, my good parents, grandmother and extended family, my sainted mother-in-law and Bill's and my children, all of whom provided me with inspiration and so many warm memories. Also deserving thanks are my teachers, mentors and friends Cynthia Richmond, Naxie Reiff, Rodger Christopherson, and Anne Seebaldt, as well as fellow members of classes and writing groups I attend who suffered through many rewrites. My dear friend Ruth Falahee read and critiqued my story in its early days. Friend Muriel Haig accompanied me to my very first writing workshop. Schoolmate and friend Margery Facklam inspired me with her many books written among and amidst her own large family. Tony De Luz, talented artist, did illustrations and cover art, formatted and submitted for publication. Others too numerous to mention also had major influences on me, my life and story, have encouraged and kept me writing since the age of eight or ten! BFK

THE WAR'S OVER, NOW GO CELEBRATE!

It was September 2nd, 1945, just past 7:00 p.m. I had only recently turned 17. Cramming for my summer session Spanish final, totally insulated from the outside world in an empty classroom at the suburban campus of the University of Buffalo, I was entirely insulated from the outside world. On the bus to the downtown campus with my nose still buried in my textbook, I never noticed the unusually heavy traffic until the driver told me, "I'll have to detour to get you there." My arrival delayed by a few minutes, I *ran* all the way to the third floor, fearful I'd be excluded for tardiness.

My fellow students standing in the hall blocked my entrance to the classroom! When I tried to ask why they weren't inside, I was abruptly shushed as an incomprehensible crackle emanated from a small radio held aloft in the doorway. "Hell! This thing's useless!" roared the professor's voice. "The office has a better radio. Follow me!" We students turned and descended the stairs after him.

Only seconds after we arrived in the first floor hallway, the announcement came loudly over the airways, "That's IT, Folks. The Japs have SURRENDERED!" I felt cold, then hot with excitement and wonder. My whole life, since Dec. 7th, 1941, had been dominated by war news. How different would life be without the war stitching patriotic purpose into everything we did? I was thrilled, but almost unbelieving. It was so difficult to comprehend!

Excitement and cheering rattled the walls. After several moments, my professor turned to the students behind him to yell hoarsely, "NO exam tonight! You all get A-A-A's! Now GO-O-O CELEBRATE!" In the ensuing exodus, I was propelled onto the sidewalk where I saw the professor head toward downtown, yelling jubilantly, "The war's over, the war's over!"

Carried along in the moving mass, I soon found myself on Main Street in downtown Buffalo, NY. But there was no street to be seen. From storefront on one side to storefront on the opposite side, it was a mass of screaming, cheering humanity. Being small, I was picked up frequently, raised aloft by exuberant celebrators, hugged and kissed by strangers. Radios in open, upstairs windows of buildings blared continuing news of the surrender. People screamed, cried, laughed, cheered, jumped up and down, hugged one another! An abandoned streetcar stood in the center of the street, locked and left by the conductor who had joined the celebrators. Farther on, a bus was abandoned, and a few cars left by their owners when the crush of people halted forward motion.

I escaped the greater mass of celebrating humanity by shoving my way through the door of a downtown office building to queue up in the long line at the lobby phone booth. Each caller entering was urged loudly, "Hurry up! Hurry up!" Finally inside the booth, I dialed home. "Bea? Where *are* you?" Dad asked, concern in his voice. When I told him, he responded, "Your mother is tied in knots worrying about you. We're hearing on the radio about the crowds in the city — you'll have a devil of a time getting home! I can't drive in to fetch you with the crush on the streets there. You'll just have to start walking away from downtown. Keep finding phone booths and call as often as you can! I'll come pick you up when you reach a place where traffic is still moving." Thumps on the door of the booth ended my call.

I began walking. At a major downtown intersection, a line of

Aussie airmen stood head and shoulders taller than the rest of the celebrants. As I neared, the first one yelled, "Cheers, Sweet'aht!" He lifted me off my feet, hugged me breathless, kissed me enthusiastically, and passed me to the next for more of the same. Handed across the intersection from one to another through what seemed an entire company of flyers, I reached the other side without once touching pavement! Plunked to the sidewalk by the last one as he reached for the next female being passed along the line, I smilingly continued making my way through the crowd. That certainly added zing to my unusual evening!

Passing through the major part of downtown, then the restaurant district, I reached the bar area, where the noisy crush of crowds was even heavier. To my surprise, right at my ear, I heard a familiar voice.

"Bea Fulton! Whatever are you doing downtown all by yourself?" I turned to see Mr. and Mrs. O'Hara, the parents of a boy I dated in high school before he enlisted with his two older brothers. Hearing the impending surrender news on the radio late that afternoon, they made their way downtown to joyfully celebrate the anticipated returns home of their sons. Leaving their car about a mile from where I met them, they continued on foot, planning to drink, make merry — and *damn the torpedoes!* They had just arrived at their destination, but when they encountered me, their parental consciences demanded they take me under their wing.

"You stay with us," I was ordered. "We'll take care of you!" They did, buying me Cokes when they ordered beers. At the first bar, they demanded the telephone from the barkeep, telling me, "You call your family to let them know we're looking after you!" Mother, aware of the O'Hara's fondness for happy parties, was worried, but Dad told me firmly over her background protests, "You stay with them! They're your best chance of getting home tonight!"

The O'Hara's finished their first drinks, urging me to "chug" my Coke. Moving from bar to bar, cheering, singing, crying, celebrating with the mob, their words became more slurred as time passed. But Mrs. O'Hara held firmly to my hand and her husband's as bulky Mr. O'Hara parted the masses in search of more celebratory beverages. Finally, he turned, happily threw his arms around his wife and me and said, blurrily, "I think I've had all-l-l the celebration I can stand … and still stand! Le's get back to the car." Mrs. O'Hara nodded. Hands remaining firmly locked, we worked our way away from downtown. At their car, I gratefully fell into the back seat and went to sleep. I knew nothing of the trip home — which may have been just as well.

In front of my parents' house, Mrs. O'Hara climbed into the back of the car to shake me awake. "Wake up, Darlin'!" she told me, pulling me out onto my feet. "When Devin comes home," she added, "he'll be so pleased we were right there to take care of you!" She quickly slipped back into the front seat as my parents and grandmother appeared silhouetted in the opened front door. I called out my thanks to their disappearing taillights as Mr. O'Hara gunned the engine. Mother and Dad came running down the walk. Throwing her arms around me, Mum exclaimed, "Oh, I've been so worried about you! Thank God you're home safe! Do you think the O'Hara's were drunk, Dear?"

"Of course they were!" my father told her. "That's why they were downtown. But they're good people. They brought her home safe and sound. We'll call tomorrow to thank them for looking after her!"

That was MY celebration of the victorious end of the war.

The following January, Willard H. Keeber, one of the outriders of the massive post-war "G.I. Invasion" of U.S. college campuses, registered at the University of Buffalo. We met there in the student union building in early 1946. His celebration of the war's end was very different from mine.

VALENTINE'S DAY, 1946

It was Valentine's Day, but it didn't matter to me. I had no special boyfriend. Tired of studying alone in the student women's lounge, I wandered into the mixed lounge looking for company. "Hey, Bea!" It was Jimmy, a classmate in my Economics course. "C'mere! I want you to meet this guy."

With Jimmy was a brown-haired man with an appealing smile. Jimmy's words tumbled over one another. "Bea, this is Will. Will, this is Bea. Will's in my chem class, Bea — he's one of the new vets here. He just got out of the Army last Thanksgiving. I'm sure you two have a lot in common." Then he added breathlessly, "Gotta run!" — and he did, after a particularly pretty classmate.

My attention was immediately captured. Looking into those smiling brown eyes — which seemed to lock onto mine and hold me prisoner! — I had the feeling I was falling into warm dark maple syrup. Collecting myself, I managed to ask, "What's your major, Will?" "Chemistry. I plan to go into research. What's yours?" "English. But I'm taking foreign languages as electives because I want to work overseas somewhere. I'm in the Work Study Program." "What's that?" he asked. "It's a kind of scholarship. I get a discount on my tuition, work part-time through university referrals, and pay as I go instead of in advance." "I'm really lucky," Will said. "Uncle Sam's paying all my tuition on this G.I. Bill. — Do you have to leave soon to go to work?" "No, there's nothing available for me today."

"That's great luck for *me*!" Will exclaimed. "Can you sit down and talk awhile?" "With this load of books I'm carrying, I'd love to sit down! I'm waiting for my friend Betty to finish her last class so we can ride home together on the bus." Gratefully, I sank into the nearest lounge chair, dropping my book bag off my shoulder. Kicking off one loafer to tuck my foot under me, I kicked the shoe beneath my chair with the other foot. Will took a chair facing mine. He was so good-looking, I felt a bit flustered, but I found conversation with him easy.

We were each only children. We both had aunts, uncles and cousins, but Will's lived in the New York City area. Mine were local — part of my life. Two cousins, also vets, were then at the University with me. I had expected to be the first in my family to graduate from college, but I told Will my cousins' accelerated programs would propel them to that milestone well ahead of me.

"I'm taking extra credits, too," Will told me. "I want to get going on my career as soon as possible." I can't do that," I told him. "My scholarship limits me to a standard schedule to allow time for both study and work. But I did earn some college credits at the evening campus while I was in high school, so at least I started a few credits ahead."

Will and I each loved to read. We confessed we weren't good at newer, faster dances, but enjoyed slow dancing to popular romantic tunes. We both liked semi-classical, jazz, and Big Band music.

Before we had time to explore other interests, Will asked, "Will you wait for me while I go get my books? I left them in the men's lounge." I agreed, so he shortcut his way behind my chair. Returning quickly, he set his books on the floor. "Hey!" Will said. "I found two movie passes in my vets' welcome bag. Would you go to a movie with me Friday? Is there anything special you'd like to see?" "I'd love to," I told him, thrilled to have him ask me for a date, " but with all the hours I've been working and studying, I don't even know what's playing." "Let's see," he said, reaching for a discarded newspaper on a nearby chair. We chose one together so I gave him my address and phone number.

"In which theater of the war did you serve, Will?" I asked him. "I was in Europe," he replied, then fell silent. To re-start the conversation, I queried, "How long were you overseas?" "Not all that long, really," he said. "I was in the 106th Infantry. We arrived on line just five days before the German breakthrough in the Battle of the Bulge. That happened December 16th, '44.

"The next two companies of my regiment were all taken prisoner." Another pause. Prompting again, I asked, "What happened to *you* then?" "It was dark when what sounded like hundreds of German tanks came roaring through. My company just had to scatter! We hadn't yet been fully provisioned with enough winter clothing or our full complement of arms and ammo. " After a moment of silence, Will went on. " … I ended up behind enemy lines with a few others." Wide-eyed, I asked, "How did you get back to your company?"

"I didn't — for a long time. We wandered around the Ardennes for weeks, dodging falling trees, Germans and artillery fire. It was pretty cold and there was no shelter except disabled tanks and trucks. But after a while, we ran across an American tank unit and were sent to the hospital." "Hospital! Were you wounded?" I asked. "Only frozen feet," Will replied off-handedly. "They treated 'em and sent me right back to duty."

Will changed the subject. "You know, the Vets' Welcome Dance is the Friday after next. Would you go to *that* with me?" I agreed to a second date. Before long he added, "There's a really nice little place to go dancing out near Chestnut Ridge Park. It's called the Chestnut Lodge. On weekends, they have a small band instead of just the juke box." He asked, "Would you go there with me the Saturday after the vets' dance?"

Just then, I saw Betty at the door. Waving to her, I made a quick decision. "Yes, I'd like that," I said, standing quickly to shoulder my book bag. "But there's Betty. I have to leave *right now* to catch our bus." "You can't go yet!" Will exclaimed. "I have to get your shoe from the men's lounge! When I went for my books, I snitched it from under your chair to keep you here long enough to ask you for some dates … I hope you won't be mad," he called over his shoulder as he ran to retrieve it. I wasn't. I was pleased Will wanted to detain me.

Breathlessly returning my shoe, he told me, "I'll be at your house at 6:15 Friday. Don't forget now!" "I won't," I promised, wiggling my foot into my shoe and turning to run for the door; the suburban bus ran on a tight schedule. "Oh!" he called after me — will you please call me Bill? That's what everyone called me in the Army. Will's my dad's name."

Betty and I just barely caught the bus. "Who was that guy you were talking to?" Betty asked breathlessly as she took a seat. "His name's … Bill," I told her, sliding in beside her. "He asked me for three dates." "*Three dates!*" Betty exclaimed. "What if you don't like him after the first one?" Unknowingly prophetic, I answered, "I think I will like him. He seems really nice."

FIRST DATE

The short time 'til Friday seemed like forever! Bill arrived at my door five minutes early.

My parents expected my new dates to come in to chat a bit so they could size them up. If they were less than approving, they suggested that instead of going out, we dance downstairs to their old Victrola. Then they came down with refreshments and stayed to visit. Those dates usually ended early! But they obviously liked Bill. They told us we'd better hurry to be on time for our movie.

I can't recall what was playing that night. As the film began to roll, Bill slid his arm along the back of my seat, lightly resting his fingertips on my shoulder. That touch ran through me like an electric shock! I spent the rest of the movie surreptitiously admiring his bony profile by the flickering light from the screen. I thought his strong, craggy face, his dark, maple-syrup eyes, brown hair, carved cheekbones and nose were so handsome! Once, while I was stealing another look at him, Bill turned to look at me, smiling when our eyes met. His hand on my shoulder moved down to give my arm a warmer touch and a gentle squeeze.

After the movie, there was still time before my curfew, so we stopped for a soda at the corner drugstore near my house. The lights and sparkling chrome were a bright contrast to the darkened theater. A young soda jerk was polishing the equipment as we chose a pair of chrome and red leatherette stools at the long marble counter. Big ears supporting his jaunty white cap, he turned eagerly to take our orders. Bill asked for a tall cola and I chose a Black Cow — a luscious concoction of root beer and vanilla ice cream … but I preferred it with chocolate ice cream.

With the soda dispenser whishing in the background, I asked Bill, "Will you tell me more about your experiences in Europe during the war?" He hesitated a moment, then nodded.

"About 38 German divisions made a surprise attack under cover of heavy fog along a 50-mile front. We had to scramble out of their way really fast! I only had time to grab my M-1 — that's a carbine, a good one, very accurate! — and a couple of ration packs before our place was smashed flat. The other guys I met up with had a couple of rations each like me, but they only had pistols. If we'd run across well-equipped German infantry troops, everything we had together wouldn't have been worth zip! But we mostly heard 'em instead of seeing 'em 'cause tanks make a lot of noise. There *were* enemy snipers around, though, so we had to watch out for *them*. They were out for blood …" Then, with clear satisfaction, "But we didn't lose any of *our* men to them!'"

From Bill's bare telling, I would never have understood the very real threat those casually mentioned snipers represented if it hadn't been for a moment over a half-century later. Dawn light was just beginning to creep around our bedroom blinds when Bill startled and sat straight up. He warned in a loud whisper, "Sniper! Get down! I'll take 'im!" Startled awake, I sat bolt upright but Bill's hand reached out reflexively to shove me down. Looking across the room, he raised both arms, then dropped his gaze, lowered his arms, exhaled loudly, fell back on his pillow — and was asleep again instantly. I lay awake thinking of him at just 19 with his own and his fellow soldiers' lives constantly at risk from enemy snipers.

On that first date, Bill went on to tell me how cold it had been in the Ardennes that winter. I knew from news reports that year had been the coldest winter in recorded European weather history! With no shelter and not enough warm clothing, Bill's small band decided they'd just have to keep moving to try to stay warm. But it wasn't long till they were chilled deep into the marrow of their bones. "However did you manage to keep from actually freezing?" I asked. "Like I said, we made it a point to stay on the move," Bill said. "We only slept in snatches — half of us at a time, just for a few minutes — then we moved on to keep our blood moving. A lot of wounded guys froze to death right there in the snow before any medics could get to them. Others just gave up and lay down to sleep when they got too cold and tired. Of course, they froze to death, too — while they slept." I felt a cold shiver up my spine. The soda jerk was moving closer and closer, absently polishing the counter, edging nearer to catch every word.

Bill looked off to a place far from the soda fountain. "After a few days, we had to start stripping clothes off bodies frozen in the snow—hats, scarves, gloves, jackets. Those clothes weren't going to help those guys anymore, so we made ourselves take them." I shuddered inside but tried not to show it. The soda jerk wasn't even remembering to polish as he listened. "I can't imagine how you survived all that!" I exclaimed.

"There wasn't that much to it," he shrugged. "We just had to think smarter and shoot straighter than the other guys. It felt like one of those nightmares that seem to go on forever. Once in a while, one of the guys actually fell asleep walking. We had to wake him up when he started to stagger so he wouldn't bang into a tree. Anyway, we needed all eyes peeled for snipers. All we kept thinking about was moving, moving, moving — and, of course, how hungry we were."

My fascination with this still-gaunt man's spare, factual story kept me riveted to his every word. I had been turned off by some vets' bragging accounts about how they won the war single handed, but Bill's simple account was so different. "What did you do about food?" I asked him. "You said you only had time to grab a couple of rations when the breakthrough happened."

"They did run out pretty fast," Bill recalled. "But a couple days out, we found a disabled German tank with some rations inside ... Funny!" he added. "My Mom's a good German cook so I thought *their* rations would taste OK, but they were just as bad as American ones!"

"You said you were out there quite a while," I said. "Surely the rations you brought along and what you found in that tank weren't enough!" "No, you're right," Bill admitted. After another pause, he continued, his voice a little quieter. "We ended up having to take rations off bodies, too — Germans *and* Americans. One of our guys couldn't open the first American rations we took from frozen G.I.'s, but another man told him, 'These won't do dead men any good, but they might just help us stay alive long enough to get out of here.' So he did eat some. None of us liked it, but we had to do it." The soda jerk was still as a statue, listening in awe.

Bill was silent again for a minute. Then he added, "I'm not sure which was the worst — being cold all the time or always being hungry." "It must have been unbearable," I exclaimed. "I don't know how you did it!" Bill thought about that for a minute. "There wasn't any choice," he said flatly. I was quiet, considering that bitter truth.

Bill was silent, his mind still in the Ardennes. Then, suddenly, he looked at his watch and said, "Hey, it's getting close to your curfew. I need to get you home on time!" He jumped off his stool and wrapped his arms around me to lift me off mine. I thought momentarily of jumping back on it so he'd put his arms around me again, but of course I didn't. Bill paid the chit and a tip and casually threw his arm around my shoulder to walk out, the soda jerk watching him with clear hero worship. I slid quickly into the car, shivering as I thought of soldiers in that frigid winter of '44-'45 without enough clothing to keep them warm.

In the car, Bill was pensive. "You know, I feel bad about how hard this was on my folks — I never thought of that when I enlisted. When they heard I was missing in action — I think that's when my mom's hair started turning gray. And Dad's a champion worrier anytime, but when he has something specific to worry about, he goes right into high gear. While I was on the ship coming home, he had a stroke … I guess I'll always wonder if he'd have had that stroke if I hadn't come up missing."

Just then, Bill braked in front of my house and turned off the engine. I turned to tell him I enjoyed the evening with him but didn't have the chance. Bill reached past the gearshift to wrap his arms around me and kiss me, a first-date sort of kiss — sweet and a little questioning. I would have liked another, but he jumped out to open the car door for me and walk me to my front porch.

There, Bill put his arms around me again, kissed me softly and said, "I can't *wait* for the vets' dance next week!" He closed his eyes and added, almost as if the thought surprised him, "I'll be thinking about you *so much* till then!" Mother opened the door from inside just then, so Bill said, "I think I brought her home on time, Mrs. Fulton." Mother smiled and nodded sleepily. He turned and strolled jauntily down the walk, whistling, and waved to me before he stepped into the car.

Mother asked me, "What did you think of that young man?" Surprising Mother, my heart spoke for me. I replied dreamily, "That's the man I'm going to marry," sighing hopefully, " … if only he'll ask me." Before Mum could say a word, I drifted upstairs to dream of Bill's strong arms and more kisses I hoped for in the future.

SODA FOUNTAIN

At 8:00 p.m. the next evening, the phone rang. I was delighted to hear Bill's voice. "Hi!" he said cheerfully. "Hi, yourself," I answered. There was a short silence, then "I was wondering … if it's not too late … well, you see, I finished my homework pretty fast and I kinda thought … if you aren't too busy, that is … maybe I could come out there. It would only take me 35 or 40 minutes to get there! We could go back to that soda fountain and talk some more. I really want to get to know you better … if you're not too busy, that is."

I had been thinking about Bill all day. My studies received divided attention as I thought more about him than the work I was laboring through. "I'm not too busy!" I told Bill. "I'd love that!"

"Good!" he answered. "I'll be there as fast as I can!" The connection clicked as he hung up without even waiting for me to say goodbye. Bill arrived on my doorstep exactly 35 minutes later. After saying hello to my folks, he turned to me, smiling, "Ready? You wouldn't want to keep a Black Cow waiting!"

At the drugstore, we chose two stools and smiled a little self-consciously at each other. The same soda jerk was clearly thrilled to see Bill again. Bill asked me, "Same as before?" I nodded, so he ordered, "One tall Coke and a Black Cow with *chocolate* ice cream." He turned to me then. "I talked too much last night. I really want to know so much more about *you*, the things you've been doing in your life — *all* that!"

I was pleased with his interest, but not sure what to tell him. "You already know I like to read. But my existence during the war was pretty tame compared to yours." "That's alright," he said. "I had a *lot* of excitement and, believe me! … it's very overrated. I'm really interested in what was going on here at home — what *you* were doing, in particular." The soda jerk delivered our order and turned back to his polishing.

I felt shy with Bill's intent eyes on mine. "What can I tell you? … Well, I fought the 'battle of the pen' a lot." "What's that?" Bill asked. "We girls were told it was our patriotic duty to let the boys overseas know they weren't forgotten back home. Names were given out at school and church, even in the newspaper — we were encouraged to write to as many servicemen as we could. Of course, I wrote to my cousins and boys at school, too, so I spent a lot of time writing."

"Not forgotten at home," Bill mused, putting his hand on my left one resting on the counter. "I'm surprised they didn't all come rushing to your door right after the war!" "Well, some of them didn't live nearby, but I went out with a couple from this area." "Are you still dating them?" Bill asked, his grip on my hand a little tighter. "Nope. After a couple of dates, we didn't really click, I guess." "Well, I'm glad of *that*!" Bill said, squeezing my hand emphatically. I set my Black Cow on the counter to drop my right hand down beside me where I could cross my fingers unseen, hoping Bill might be as interested in me as I was in him. "Tell me what else you did here at home!" he urged.

After picking up my soda for another sip, I recalled, "I *hated* weeding the Victory garden!" "Victory garden?" Bill asked, "What's that?" I was amazed; they were such a part of civilian life during the war! "People were urged to plant edibles to reduce the drain on farm produce," I explained, "to free farmers to enlist. Kale and chard are supposed to be very good for you, and of course, we ate what we grew, but I hated both of them!"

Then I asked him, "Will you tell me more about what happened to you in Europe?" The soda jerk looked up. "I will, another time," Bill promised. "But first I want to hear more about what was happening here at home – with *you*, that is."

"Well, let's see — there were the nightly black-outs in case of air raids, with all the windows covered and volunteer wardens patrolling to be sure no sliver of light showed outdoors. If I had to come home after dark, Mum and Dad insisted I run the six houses from the bus! And I'd *better* get home breathless or face a lecture! ... Then there were ration cards for things like flour and sugar and meat. That was to free farmers, too." "Yeah, I forgot about that! I remember getting ration cards before I enlisted," Bill told me.

"Gas rationing was really important," I recalled. "Posters everywhere asked, 'Is this trip necessary?' We rode bikes a lot — even for dates here at the soda fountain or anyplace nearby."

"Things must have been very different from before the war," Bill observed. "Mom and Dad never wrote about any of that." "I'm sure they *didn't*! Most of us here at home wouldn't even *think* about writing anything to servicemen that might sound like complaining. We tried to do anything we thought might help the war effort, even just dealing as cheerfully as possible with annoyances. Compared with what you guys were doing, it was so little!" I told him.

"Tell me more about how things were here at home, will you?" Bill asked.

"Well, I guess I can admit *now* that shoe rationing was a pain," I recalled. "I have narrow feet — " "I can see," Bill said, "and they look really nice, not big tugboats like a lot of girls." "Thank you," I replied, glad I'd switched from my penny loafers to heels after Bill called, "but shoe rationing is definitely a negative recollection for me. They don't make many narrows to begin with and there were even fewer then. I always kept hoping for pretty shoes the next time I had enough coupons saved up. But it always seemed the only ones that fit me were the ugly ones! I used to call them my 'ugly-mugglies'!"

"You look very nice in what you're wearing tonight," Bill observed. "There ARE more narrows available these days," I answered, feeling the warmth of a blush. Then I asked, "Why don't you tell me more about how you survived behind enemy lines? I'd really like to hear more about that." The soda jerk's attention immediately focused on Bill.

"There really wasn't that much to it. Like I said, we just had to think better and shoot straighter than the other guys ... But I still want to hear more about the sorts of things *you* did here at home." The soda jerk looked disappointed.

"Well-l-l, maybe sometime you'd get a laugh out of my experiences at my rifle club. "You belong to a rifle club?" Bill exclaimed. "Not now, but there was one at my high school the semester after Pearl Harbor. — But look, it's going on 10:00 already! I'm supposed to help in the church nursery at the first service tomorrow. Mum and Dad have to be up, too, to drive me, so I'd better not stay out too late. "

When he pulled up in front of my house, Bill kissed me goodnight, then heaved a sigh. "I have a lot of homework and a couple of exams this week, so I don't think I can see you again till the Vets' Dance next Friday." Disappointed, I answered a little flippantly, "Well, then, we'll just have to wait 'til Friday, won't we?" "May I call you evenings?" Bill asked quickly. "Sure," I told him, still a little nettled. "I'll be home some evenings, but not all of them!" careful not to mention that my only planned evening out was for a sorority meeting. After a thoughtful moment, Bill said firmly, "I'll *definitely* be calling you!"

He did, making arrangements to meet me three times that week for lunch in the Student Union cafeteria when our schedules coincided. After that, by unspoken agreement, we continued to meet there those days.

STUDENT UNION LUNCHES

Eager to know one another better, we talked steadily at those lunches. At the first one, Bill was determined to hear more about that rifle club.

"Right after Pearl Harbor," I told him, "a lot of the senior boys enlisted immediately. Juniors were disappointed they weren't old enough, so they spent a lot of time talking about the war and neglecting their schoolwork. The boys' advisor at school thought of starting an after-school rifle club to help them feel they were at least preparing themselves for the Service. Only one of the teachers knew anything about guns. He grew up on a farm shooting wild turkeys and 'varmints' he said bothered the stock. He borrowed some guns for it from his hunting friends. A B average was required to belong, so the boys got back to their schoolwork so they could join."

"But what did that have to do with you?" Bill wanted to know. "Well, I *did* have a B average. I'd never even held a gun, but I thought I'd like to try it. They didn't say girls *couldn't* join, so I went out to the far end of the football field where they met.

"I *was* the only girl there. When I showed up, the boys poked fun at me, asking if I wanted to learn how to get a guy with a gun. The teacher looked kind of amused, too." "That wasn't very nice of them," Bill observed."

"That's what I thought!" I told him, " — but I wasn't going to let them chase me off before I tried it out, so I asked the teacher how to get started. He was grinning, but he showed me how to get down on one knee to hold the rifle, then he told me to go ahead and shoot at the target." "How did you do?" Bill asked. "I didn't hit anything *then*, except maybe the sky. The teacher hadn't told me about the recoil, so it knocked me right over. The boys thought that was *really* funny …" "That was ungentlemanly of them!" Bill exclaimed, "and that teacher, too!" "I thought so, too!" I agreed. "My shoulder hurt, but it made me sort of mad, so I just got up and dusted myself off. 'That was a real jolt!' I told the teacher. 'Is there a way to avoid that the next time?'"

"Good for you!" Bill was smiling. "What did he do then?" He looked a little embarrassed and told the boys to stop their cackling. Then he showed me the right way to snuggle the stock into my shoulder. He told me to shoot it again and I was really surprised when I hit the target! It was way off near the edge, but at least I hit it." "I'll bet that showed 'em!" Bill said, smiling. "They didn't say anything then, but when I hit it again on my next try — even way out on the edge — a couple of them clapped and the teacher told me, 'Well done!' He sounded really surprised.

"It took a couple of weeks before they accepted me. When I hit a little bit in from the edge of the target, a few of them clapped again. Then, at the next meeting, I nicked the edge of the bull's eye on my first try! They *all* cheered and slapped my back. When I got more good hits as the meetings went on, they started to tease me again, but in a friendlier way — they began calling me 'Annie,' for that woman in those famous Wild West shows. I really did enjoy target practice."

"Well, it sounds as if you certainly had a knack for it!" Bill injected.

"I don't know about that, but I always go after anything new like it's a race for my life. After several meetings, I met the teacher's qualifications for 'Marksman' — he said he based it on the Army's requirements." "Really?" Bill exclaimed with a smile, "That's VERY good!"

"I never had the chance to aim for higher ratings, though," I told Bill, "because the rifle club only met that one semester. The teacher himself enlisted at the end of the term, and there were no other teachers who knew anything about firearms. But it was fun while it lasted."

"Well, I'm impressed!" Bill told me, smiling. It wasn't a make-fun-of-me-smile, either. It was a nice one.

"But the sad part about it," I remembered somberly, "was in our senior year when we heard the teacher had been killed in action. I felt really bad then."

During other lunchtimes together, we told each other about our families. Bill was proud of his folks, and from what he told me about them, I thought he had good reason for that.

Both of them were orphaned at 17, and managed to support themselves and thrive. Bill's mom came here alone from Germany, while Bill's dad's family, of German extraction, had been in the U.S since his grandfather — an immigrant — fought in the Mexican and Civil wars.

Bill told me his parents were a lot older than mine. He said his mom once told him that his dad was so determined to save a lot of money before he dared propose to her that she despaired of his *ever* getting around to popping the question!

When Bill asked about my family, I told him my mom came here from London at 11 years of age when her mother, a new widow, brought her family of five children to the U.S. in hopes they could do better here without a father than in England. My dad was a Scottish immigrant who came here at 20, after four years of military service in World War I. Bill was interested to learn that my dad also served in the Ardennes Forest, just as Bill did.

We talked about our interests, too. Bill was good at math, and really enjoyed the subject. I was terrible at it; I told him my dad unsuccessfully tried to bring me up to speed with evening tutoring. Dad had taken correspondence college courses to become an accountant after which he worked at the Erie County Auditor's Office. He really enjoyed working with figures. But for me, it was torture just getting through enough math to qualify for my college entrance diploma!

Bill asked what I *did* like. When I told him enthusiastically, "Foreign languages!" he told me he was really bad at that sort of thing and hoped he wouldn't need any languages to qualify for his degree in Chemistry or his minor in Math. We both enjoyed English Lit, though.

Somehow, after those lunches, I managed to pay attention to my professors, but it was really hard for me to keep my thoughts from dwelling on Bill.

THE VETS' WELCOME DANCE

"Will you *look* at all the cars here? Every vet at UB must be here!" Bill exclaimed as we pulled into the parking lot. I had to work late that afternoon, so the dance was in full swing when we arrived at the student union for the second of the dates Bill made with me the day we met. He quickly swung me onto the floor, holding me close. "This is going to be so great!" he told me. "I've been looking forward to this all week!" "I have, too," I admitted.

Just then, another veteran tapped Bill on the shoulder to ask, "Cut?" Bill dropped his arms in surprise, and the man's dance partner put her hand on Bill's shoulder expectantly as the man quickly danced me away. Couples were joining, separating, taking new partners, separating again, and dancing away with still others. When Bill next caught sight of me, he plowed his way determinedly across the floor to claim and dance me away.

He immediately asked, "How about stopping for refreshments?" I agreed just as his shoulder was tapped again. "We're going for some food!" he stated firmly. We chose some goodies, but before we finished our refreshments, Bill had a better idea. "What would you think about getting out of here?" he asked, " — and just going for a ride somewhere?" I nodded, eager to spend more time alone with him.

"I didn't realize that a 'welcome' dance' would be for vets to meet as many coeds as possible!" he told me ruefully as we walked toward the car. "I guess that *was* the idea," I agreed. "But I only wanted to dance with YOU!" he protested as he opened the car door for me.

"How about something hot to drink?" Bill asked when he spotted a diner near the university. I nodded, told him that sounded good. Patrons were lined up at the counter for their orders. "What would you like?" he asked me. "Hot chocolate, please," I told him.

When he brought our drinks to the booth I claimed, I had to blow on mine before I could swallow it. Bill sipped his without wincing. I teased him, "You'd make a good devil the way you handle that heat!" He smiled. "Then you must be an angel, since you have to blow on yours!" he replied. "But that's good; every devil needs an angel to steer him right." Suddenly, I felt a lot warmer than my first sip of chocolate warranted.

"You promised to tell me more about how you survived behind enemy lines. I'd really like to hear more about that," I told him. Bill nodded with a very serious look, but after a few seconds' silence, he brightened and asked, "Would you like to go back to your house and dance a little there?" I had told him about the Victrola in the basement we escaped on our first date. "I was really looking forward to dancing with you tonight," he added hopefully. "Sure, let's do that!" I told him.

DANCING AT HOME

Mum and Dad brought a plate of cookies and some lemonade downstairs while we chose records and started the first one turning. But then they left us to ourselves to dance dreamily to the music. After dancing to a few, Bill put on a new one, but instead of taking me in his arms to dance, he took my elbow and led me to the old couch against the wall.

Bill wrapped his arms around me. His kiss was sweet and lingering. Bill was so handsome and he wore the mantle of heroism so casually. His gaunt, bony face bore testimony to the trials he endured. After hesitating barely a mini-second there on the old couch, I kissed him back willingly. The record played on but we paid it no attention.

I learned later that Bill was actually a cautious man, used to carefully considering his own actions as well as the expected reactions. Certainly his experiences in the war encouraged his natural built-in caution — except where I was concerned. There (Bill told me long afterwards), he found his emotions racing ahead like a runaway freight train. He surprised himself with his own instant ardor, but he was as powerless to stop that train as I was.

Our kisses rapidly became more and more passionate. The record ended, but we didn't notice until I heard Mother's footsteps in the kitchen and pulled away from Bill's arms. In as collected a voice as I could summon, I urged him, "Tell me more about that American tank unit, will you?" Bill sat back, changing gears. "Yeah, they *SURE* saved our sorry hides," he acknowledged. "But before that happened, we had one *really good* day!"

Amazed, I asked, "What was so good about it? What happened then? Weren't you still in German territory?" Mother's footsteps returned to the living room after hearing us in conversation.

"Yeah, we were," Bill said, "But that morning, the clouds finally cleared away and it was so cheerful to see the sun for a change!" Bill pulled me close to him again as he went on. My breath felt trapped in my chest, but I tried to ignore it. "It was the first time since the breakthrough and all that awful weather that aircraft were able get up in the air. The whole sky was filled with it! At first, they were all German planes, so we weren't happy to see *them*. But THEN," he exulted, "along came hundreds and hundreds of American and Allied planes!

"They kept coming and coming and *coming* all day long — I never saw that many planes in the air in my whole life! When we saw our own aircraft up there, we jumped up and down and cheered and hollered till we were hoarse. Then we dragged our tails on some more till one of the guys looked up and started to holler again, so we all stopped to yell and cheer some more. We were so excited to see our own guys up there! Before that day, we kept forcing ourselves along. None of us dared say we were worried we might not make it out alive, but it was hard to feel real sure about it, passing so many other dead GI's in the snow. You couldn't help wondering if you'd end up like them. But THAT day I think we all actually began to feel kind of hopeful!"

I remembered reading about that first fly-day. It was all over the papers. "When did that happen?" I asked Bill.

"I think it was about Christmastime," Bill told me." "But weren't you still behind German lines?" I asked. "I think so." Bill considered the question. " — But the tanks were the big operators at that time and they were pushing each other back and forth, so the line was pretty flexible about then, I guess."

Bill put his finger under my chin and tilted it up to kiss me again. I reached my arms around his neck to kiss him back. He went on after the kiss, still holding me in his arms. "One day maybe a week after that, we were slogging along as usual, listening to our stomachs complain, when we heard tanks again. Of course, we dodged off the track to find cover. But when we saw it was an American unit, not more Germans, we sort of went nuts! We ran out and jumped up and down and waved and yelled as loud as we could — and they *saw* us!" At that, Bill's arm tightened around me. I tried to melt into his nearness. "You know, they didn't have much peripheral visibility in those big cans. We were so lucky they saw us! They stopped and piled out to talk to us. They were really surprised to hear our story. They kept saying, 'You've really been out here ever since the breakthrough? And you didn't lose *any* of your men? — Wow!' We were amazed they were so surprised. We'd just slogged along every day because we didn't have any other choice."

Bill responded to my unspoken wish and stopped to kiss me again — at first gently, then more insistently. He looked up as if expecting to hear Mother's footsteps again, but held me close as he resumed his story, speaking directly into my ear.

"A Lieutenant ordered them to make room for us on board several of the tanks. They were pretty crowded in them, but they managed to squeeze us in. They were on their way back from an unsuccessful scouting trip searching for Nazi units." At that, Bill sat up straighter, leaving his arm around my shoulder. "They were almost as excited about rescuing us as we were to be rescued. They said they at least accomplished *something* worthwhile in their night's work by cheating the Nazis out of our miserable, drag-tail little bunch of doughboys!" Bill kissed me again, but that time it was a resounding kiss, as if celebrating being saved! However he kissed me was all right with me, just so long as he kissed me. I felt like clay, trying to meld with his every mood.

"What happened to you after they picked you up?" I asked when I could catch my breath. "Where did they take you?" My voice was a little shaky both from the kiss and from better realizing what a terrible experience Bill had survived — hearing about the tank crew's astonishment. Bill was only three years older than me right then, and he'd been in the Ardennes just a year or so earlier. I didn't think I could possibly have made it through had I been in his shoes! So many others had just given up and died in that awful year's snow and cold. The truth behind Bill's matter-of-fact account was clear. It was only dogged determination and heroism that pulled him and his fellows through!

"They took us to their base. As soon as we got there, their Major talked with each one of us alone. He recorded our names and ranks and asked for our accounts of what happened to us. I suppose it was so a report could be sent to our families that we weren't still missing. After that, he got on the horn and radioed somewhere else. Pretty soon, medics came rushing up in Jeeps. They looked us over, then they loaded us into their vehicles to take us to a nearby American field hospital.

"Most of the tank crew came out to cheer for us when the medics drove us out, including the Lieutenant who ordered them to take us on board — and their Major came out, too, and saluted as we passed him!" Bill fell silent, remembering. His expression proved that part of his recollection was a very good memory. He kissed me — a very celebratory kiss as he re-lived that highlight!

"You said they treated you for frozen feet, " I noted, hoping for more of that story, content to have him talk on with me in his arms. "Well, not right then." Bill sat up, removed his arm from my shoulder, took my hand and began to stroke it thoughtfully. He looked up at the old clock on the wall. "It's almost your curfew time," he said regretfully, "so I'd better get going soon. But let's dance a little more before I leave." I nodded soberly, surprised at how quickly the time had passed. Bill stood up to put on another record. We danced to that one, then Bill piled up the records on the shelf. I started toward the stairs. "Wait!" Bill said. I turned back to find him right behind me. He wrapped his arms tightly around me. "You're not only pretty and nice," he whispered into my ear, "but you're a really gutsy lady to listen through all this." He kissed me again, not a quick one, not a sweet one, but a long, lingering, insistent one. I kissed him back willingly. He held me a little away from him to look right into my eyes. "You're the best thing that's ever happened to me!" he declared shakily. I didn't want to move but Bill said, "We need to go upstairs now or your folks might not let me come back. And I don't want *that* to happen." He released me from his arms and turned me toward the stairs. "Don't forget," he said, as he followed me up the steps, "You're going with me to the Chestnut Lodge tomorrow night." "I know," I said. "I'm looking forward to it." "Me, too!" Bill answered.

Bill thanked my parents for putting up with him after what he called our "escape" from the vets' welcome dance. "It was too crazy!" he told them. "It was a whole lot better just dancing and talking quietly here." Mum and Dad were smiling as he turned to leave. "How about if I pick you up tomorrow at 7:30?" Bill asked. I nodded and said I'd be ready then. I stood at the door watching him walk to the car, whistling.

CHESTNUT LODGE

The next evening, Bill was a little early again. I wasn't quite finished gussying up in a pretty dress and my three-inch heels. When I walked into the living room, Bill let out a long, low whistle. I couldn't resist twirling around so my skirt flirted out around me. "You look like dessert! … Doesn't she?" Bill added, turning to my father. Dad laughed and said, "She looks nice to me, too. You two go along now and have a good time." Bill asked my father for my curfew time, but Dad waved his hand dismissively. "Just don't make it too late," he said. It was clear he and Mother liked Bill.

The Chestnut Lodge was a little way out into the countryside — a small dance place. Bill wheeled directly into what seemed to be the only parking space left. We hurried to the door with the cold wind poking icy fingers into our collars.

"The Lodge," as we came to call it, had a warm, cozy feeling with a band at one side of the room, a small dancing area and closely spaced, candlelit tables. A hostess led us to a table just beside the dance floor. We watched the other dancers as we quietly sipped our first drinks, warming up after the chill wind.

When Bill asked if I wanted to dance, I nodded. He was silent as we moved to the smooth rhythms of the band. I rested my head on his shoulder where I could hear his heart beating strongly, relieved he couldn't hear mine since it was playing such a happy telltale staccato. The music ended just as we reached our own table. Bill tilted his head toward it and raised an eyebrow questioningly. I shook my head, so he held me close again as the music resumed. I can't remember how many tunes were played before we sat down. The ice cube remaining in my glass had melted by then and the waiter appeared to ask, "Another round?" I took a swallow of water, thought about it momentarily, and decided, "Actually, I'd like a ginger ale now." Bill asked for the same.

I turned to Bill to remind him, "You know, you've still never told me anything about that hospital overseas." "I guess I didn't," he replied. "But you haven't told me anything about how you happened to be there in the student lounge where we met. What was it that brought *you* to the University?"

"I'd always planned on college, for as long as I recall," I told him. "Mum and Dad both read voraciously, and once I learned how, I did, too! All through school, I read everything I could lay my hands on, so it was just assumed I'd go on to college. *And* find a way to earn a scholarship because I always knew Dad and Mum couldn't pay my way."

"I never even thought about going to college," Bill told me. "I just expected to get a job after high school like most guys in my neighborhood. Then, I enlisted when I found out I could sign up to go into an officer training program at Syracuse University. In fact, that only lasted one semester before the African campaign took so many men that the Army needed more boots on the ground in a hurry. We were all transferred into the Infantry as buck Privates. So much for officer training! My Mom was always going on about how people should "better themselves" any way they can, so with the G.I. Bill available to me after the war, I jumped at the chance for a college education!"

Bill went on, "*You* mentioned taking college classes while you were still in high school. I didn't know you could do that. How did that work?" "I just signed up for evening courses and paid the tuition," I replied. "I had money saved toward college from babysitting and summer work. The university could only award 'pass' grades 'til after I graduated from high school. But after that, I was able to start college this Fall with official credit hours for the B grades I earned. I think having those early credits probably helped me to be named for my Work Study Scholarship."

"You must be pretty smart to pass college courses before you were even out of high school!" Bill observed. "I don't think it's a matter of 'smart' so much as interested," I replied. "Well, *I* think it's a matter of 'smart!'" Bill responded determinedly. I smiled at him and said, "OK, now it's your turn. You were going to tell me about that hospital over there."

Bill took a long swallow of his ginger ale before saying, "Fair enough." He thought a minute, then began. " ... After we were checked out at the field hospital, they loaded us into a troop carrier to take us to a larger hospital farther from the front. It was a cold ride; those tanks were warmer! When we got there, the intake non-com said they were pretty full, so they separated us and sent us to different wards." Bill felt silent for a little while, then added regretfully, "You know, I never saw any of those guys again. I didn't even know their names. We just called each other by crazy nicknames." Then he reached over to put his hand on my arm. "Let's dance again!"

As we slowly circled the floor, I asked what Bill's nickname had been. "Once in a while, they called me 'Hot-shot,'" he said, then added, "but mostly, they just called me 'M-1,' because I had the best weapon of any of us — my carbine — and I kept it right with me, ready all the time." Then Bill pushed my hair back and kissed my ear. I barely breathed, but I did nestle closer into his arms. "This is what I like most about dancing," Bill said quietly into that same ear. "You can hold a girl as close as you like and nobody thinks anything of it. Except me, that is. I've been thinking about this since our first date. And ever since last night, I couldn't think of *any*thing but holding you in my arms again!"

I didn't trust my voice. I simply left my head on Bill's shoulder. But after a couple of minutes, I looked up into those maple-syrup eyes and whispered, "Me, too." Bill smiled broadly and hugged me a little closer. The music stopped just then and the roving spotlight came to rest on us. I closed my eyes against the light and left my head on his shoulder till the music began again.

When the next dance ended, the band took a break so we returned to our table. I wasn't sure I could breathe evenly, but I tried to collect myself as we sat down. Playing for time as I felt my heart thumping erratically, I asked Bill to tell me more. "I had to give up my carbine at the hospital, but they returned it when they sent me back to my unit. — I thought of it for so long as my ticket out of there that, when they took it away, I felt naked without it!" Bill waved to the waiter, gesturing toward our ginger ales for a refill.

"I guess they finally treated your feet at that second hospital," I noted, trying hard to contact 'normal' inside myself. I didn't trust my voice to say much more than that one sentence. "Yeah," Bill answered, "but first, they gave me a *whole meal* — and it wasn't just rations! It was the first real food I'd had since before the Germans came through!" I see-sawed between the still-warm feeling of being in his arms when we danced and my shock when I realized how dangerously close to starvation Bill must have come. He smiled at me. "I really *liked* being in that hospital. Not only did they give me three meals a day with snacks in between but it was nice and warm in there!" Then his smile faded and he fell silent again. I waited.

"There was only one problem," he finally added, thoughtfully. "Every night the Krauts sent buzz bombs over, like the ones they used for the London blitz. We'd lay there in the dark listening to them shrieking overhead. If the sound kept on going, it was OK. — for us, anyway. But if the noise stopped, you knew it was coming down. That was when we all rolled off our cots and under them." A pause, then a long breath, " — except for the really badly wounded guys. They had to just lie there in their cots and wait."

The music started again, and Bill stood up to reach for my hand. We danced silently. All I could think of was men in or under their cots waiting for bombs to explode. My mind wasn't really on the dance, although I couldn't help feeling good in Bill's arms.

At the end of the first selection, Bill steered me back to our table. He put one hand on mine, reached for his ginger ale, took a long swallow, then added thoughtfully, "A funny thing happened one night. We called those things 'screaming meemies'. One of them went silent, so we automatically rolled off our cots, and I should have slid under mine. But for some reason, I thought I was back out there — being attacked. Maybe I was still asleep. They told me I kept grabbing around on my own cot and the next one for my M-1, yelling like crazy for somebody to give me back my carbine. A medic came running in to wake me up. It took a second to realize where I was. Neither of us were under cots when the explosion came — but it wasn't on top of us, anyway, so it was all right."

I couldn't say anything, imagining how terrified Bill must have been, not finding his weapon at hand when he thought he needed it — and what deadly danger he and the medic were risking with no cover while the bomb was falling! "*Was* the hospital bombed I asked him. "No," Bill answered very seriously. "We were really lucky. A few exploded nearby, but nothing hit the hospital itself. Just the same, it was nerve-wracking there in the dark when the sound stopped. It seemed like *forever*, waiting for the explosion, wondering if that one had your name on it. — Sometimes, somebody in the ward just *dreamed* another bomb was on its way down, and rolled off his cot yelling, 'Take cover!' Some of the guys would swear at him 'cause he woke them up for no good reason. With one thing and another, we didn't get much sleep. But nobody minded if we dozed a lot in the daytime." Then he brightened. "But I always woke up when they brought the food through!"

"How badly were your feet damaged?" I asked, thinking that Bill seemed able to dance all right. "They didn't exactly call it frozen feet," he answered. "They called it trench foot. That's when your feet stay cold and wet for a long time. It can cause nerve damage. Not many streams were still frozen solid because of all the tank activity. We had to wade through so much snow and water! … As far as I understood it, my feet were frozen all right, but I was lucky. I didn't lose any toes like some of the guys did, so I got off scot-free."

"Your feet must have been so cold, being wet all the time!" I commented. "Yeah," he admitted, "but sometimes we found dry boots on bodies frozen in the snow. We took 'em to replace our wet ones." Another pause, then Bill added in a subdued tone, "But we could never bring ourselves to strip the socks off those poor guys — so we still had to wear our own wet ones even when we found dry boots."

I was quiet thinking about Bill and the others having to remove clothes and boots from dead men, unable to leave their bare feet exposed to the weather. Bill stood up and reached for my hand to dance again. As I moved onto the floor in his arms, I looked up at him to ask, "How long were you at the hospital?" "I think it was about three weeks," Bill said, "but I don't exactly know. It was kinda like 'time out.' One day ran into the next. Maybe it was 'cause we only slept in snatches with those buzz bombs coming over every night."

Bill held me close, then slid his hand up from my back to gently push my head down onto his shoulder. "That's better!" he said.

"— Anyway, before they sent me off to rejoin the One-oh-sixth, the doc there told me to always keep my feet warm and dry, to always carry a pair of dry socks in my pocket and to never, *ever* stay in wet socks and shoes again for the rest of my life. Like he thought I'd *chosen* wet socks! But I did take his advice, and I always carried dry ones in a pocket after that." He chuckled a bit ruefully, then added, "The habit stuck! Believe it or not, there's a pair of them in my coat pocket right now."

For the rest of his life, whenever Bill packed for a trip, socks were the first items in his case. But he was wrong; he didn't escape "scot-free" as he thought. Much later in life, nerve damage in his feet and lower legs affected his ability to walk despite always keeping his feet dry and warm after the war.

"When you returned to your regiment, I'll bet you were glad to see men you knew again," I said, as the dance ended and we returned to our table. "Well, actually, I didn't know anybody there. If two or three of our guys turned up somewhere after the breakthrough when so many of us were reported missing, they were just reassigned to whatever unit found them if they didn't get sent to the hospital. My regiment lost so many men between those captured, the ones killed and others reassigned that it had to be cobbled back together as a unit with a bunch of newcomers. That happened just before I got out of the hospital, so there wasn't anybody in my company I remembered." He added, "Funny how the other guys never made it back to the unit, though — only me. I never figured out where they sent them."

He beckoned the waiter to order snacks. Bill ate his without much attention to what he was swallowing. Then he reached over to take my hand. "This is Saturday," he said. "I have a lot of homework to do for midterms next week. Would you save next Friday for me?" That night at the Chestnut Lodge was the last of the three dates Bill made with me the day we met. I was hoping he'd ask me for another one, so I accepted gladly. We decided to go to another movie and stop again at the soda fountain.

"Listen!" Bill said. "They're playing 'When They Begin the Beguine.' Let's make this our last dance. I want to be sure to get you home before your father decides I brought you back at an *un*reasonable hour!"

As we moved into the passing dancers with Bill holding me close, I lost track of time. Only my feet were glad to have the music stop. *They* were really complaining about those three-inch heels! When that selection ended, Bill paid the bill quickly, then hurried me to the lobby for our coats.

When he stopped at my house, Bill reached past the stick shift to take me in his arms and kiss me good night — another long, sweet, lingering kiss. I wanted it to go on forever, but he sat back and said stoically, "Well, I need to take you in and face the music!" He asked my folks a little hesitantly if we were home early enough. Despite looking a little sleepy, Dad casually laid his newspaper aside, saying, "Oh yes, this is fine. We're almost done with our reading." … I dreamed of Bill again that night, as I had begun to do regularly.

OUR FIRST NEW DATE — OF MANY MORE

The next weekend, when we stopped at the soda fountain, I asked Bill to tell me more about his time in Europe. That same soda jerk was on duty again, just as eager to hear as I was. He served us pretty quickly and moved on down the counter, but not very far.

"After I got out of the hospital," Bill began, "The Company was sent to a place where we saw some light action — nothing really intense. Then we were posted to a place on the Normandy coast in France to guard the open end of a peninsula where German troops were trapped near the sea. We didn't see *any* action there, though. I guess by then the Krauts knew the end was inevitable, so they just hung around out of our sight "til the war in Europe ended and we were moved out of there."

"I'll bet there was a lot of celebrating when the German war ended!" I said eagerly. "Well, yeah, at *first*, after we were told about it," he agreed. "That was on May 9th, '45. After an officer announced that the German High Command had surrendered, he ordered us to be at ease. There was some cheering and backslapping till we were ordered to form up again. Then he read an order for us to be shipped to the Pacific as soon as transport was available! *That* stopped the cheering right then and there! The *Germans* may have been done, but the war was still on for US as long as the Japs were still at it!"

"What happened to you next?" I asked. By then the soda jerk had his back to us, barely moving as he only occasionally remembered to swipe at the soda machine. "They kept us busy for a couple of weeks cleaning latrines and doing K.P. Then we were all shipped out of that sector and into Germany near the town of Bingen to guard a prisoner-of-war camp. I could never figure out why they bothered with it since the German war was all over then anyway. But at least we weren't being shipped to the Pacific while we had that duty!

"It was the same old thing again 'til late August or early September — latrines, KP and guard duty — pretty boring. I was walking the perimeter one day when a sergeant came roaring up in a jeep. He ordered me off-line to report in and then he drove right on. I hiked in, saw the entire unit assembling in formation, so I just took my place and waited — I told you we sure did a lot of waiting in the military!" The soda jerk and I both did the same.

Bill took a long, thoughtful drink of his Coke. "Finally, an officer came out to announce that the Japs had surrendered — and then he dismissed us. Let me <u>tell</u> you, there was some *real* yelling and cheering then! But even so, we settled down kinda soon since we still didn't know exactly what was going to happen to us next. You know, when you're in the Army, Uncle Sam *owns* you!" I was quiet as my mind flashed back to downtown Buffalo's carefree celebration just months earlier.

"A funny thing happened while all the excitement was going on," Bill added. " — Somebody unlocked the main gate! I never knew who did it, but it had to be somebody in command. Prisoners came streaming out; they were watching us pretty nervously. Maybe they expected us to shoot them down, but we were too busy cheering. As they walked on down the road, though, they looked pretty dejected despite just being set free. We didn't think anything about what *they* were going to do. After all, they were just enemy prisoners and they were nothing to us.

"But later I heard that Germany was in really bad shape. I thought about them then. It had to be a long, tough walk back for a lot of them — to wherever they came from. They had no money and no rations, just what was on their backs and their feet, so they had to scrounge in country that was pretty much worked over. A lot of them probably didn't even have homes to go back to, and maybe couldn't even find their families. I guess war's hell for ordinary doughboys no matter what side they're on." The soda jerk turned to look directly at Bill, perhaps surprised to hear him expressing sympathy for the defeated German solders. Then he caught my eye and guiltily turned back to polishing the soda machine.

"Anyway," Bill went on in answer to my next question, "after that, they kept us busy for a little while, until they transported us to someplace near Marseilles and from there to where we boarded our ship home. They just off-loaded us from the troop carriers right onto the ship, and it took off right away. You know, military transport is like you're a bunch of cattle. You never get to say anything about it, they never tell you anything, and then you're just dumped somewhere."

"But I'll bet you were glad to be heading home!" I said to him. The soda jerk was back to polishing the counter, edging closer, but Bill didn't notice him. "Let me tell you, THAT was one *great* voyage!" Bill grinned at me in recollection. "We didn't have any duties, so we just sat around and shot the breeze, listening to American dance music. At first, there was a lot of poker and craps going on. The officers mostly looked the other way if they saw it; nobody got in any real trouble for it.

"Anyway, the guys who were real good at it soon cornered all the moola, so there was no more gambling after that great money swap. We all just sat around and listened to music." Bill ran down for a minute, seemed to be looking back in time with a little smile playing at the corners of his mouth. Then he recalled, "Somebody kept playing 'Sentimental Journey' over and over, all day, every day — and most of the nights. But nobody minded, even at night. Every so often, one of the guys would start to tear up when that was playing, but everybody tried not to because if the others saw that sort of stuff, they'd razz the pants off you."

"Just when did you get out and finally get back home, then?" I asked. "Actually, I got home on leave immediately after landing in the U.S. They peeled me out right when we landed and sent me on alone from New York to Buffalo. The Red Cross was involved in that! My father had a stroke while I was at sea, so leave was granted for me to stay with him 'til he came home from the hospital. They call that a 'compassionate leave.'

"I finally arrived on base toward the end of October, just before my 21st birthday. They processed us out as fast as they could crank out the paperwork. The minute I had those discharge papers in my hand, I called collect to tell my folks. Then I was *outta* there within an hour! I was back home in Cold Spring by Thanksgiving — as a civilian, that time ... I was sure glad to get back to Mom's cooking!" Bill added appreciatively. I saw the soda jerk smile a little to himself. I did, too. "I didn't even stay long enough to pick up my medals and ribbons," Bill added. "What medals were you awarded?" I asked. The soda jerk didn't even attempt to be discreet. He looked straight at Bill expectantly. "I dunno; I didn't *care*. I just wanted to get outta there as fast as I could!" The soda jerk looked disappointed.

It was about 55 years later when our sons persuaded Bill to write to his Congressman about his medals. A bulky package was eventually delivered. I watched Bill breathlessly as he opened it. Among his various service ribbons and badges, Bill discovered a separate box containing a Bronze Star, awarded for "heroic, meritorious achievement." That tank Major's report and Bill's fellow soldiers' accounts must have been responsible. Bill never knew about it 'til then. He didn't say much when he opened the package, but he appeared quietly pleased. At first, Bill kept the box on the table beside his chair in the living room. Every so often, he'd reach over to touch it with his fingertips. Occasionally, he tapped the top, as if emphasizing a point in his mind. But after about a week, he put it with the rest of the ribbons in the top drawer of his bureau. I never saw him take any of them out again after that.

When Bill pulled up in front of my house that night after we left the soda fountain, he reached past the gearshift once more to put his arm around my shoulders and take my hand in his. "And now I'm back here getting a college education so I can have a decent career and make a good life!" he said. At that, he turned to look into my eyes and added quietly, " … and dating a beautiful girl." I swallowed hard and couldn't think of a word to say. But Bill kissed me then so there was no need for conversation. Too soon, he reached for the door handle, saying, "I'd better get you in or your folks may be out here with a shotgun."

Bill was a man who took responsibility. If he was expected to do anything, he did it. If he promised something, he kept his word. If he made a deal, he honored all parts of it. It was a matter of personal self-respect for him to do the best he could and to fulfill expectations to the best of his ability or better — and mostly, he achieved "better." He stretched himself; he reached past what he thought his capability. He listened to ideas and considered them. He was willing to adopt them or a version of them if they seemed logical to him. He learned and re-learned all his life. Except for relating a couple of amusing incidents from the war, that was almost the last Bill ever spoke of it — it was over and done with. He always focused on facing forward — toward the rest of his life.

THE COURSE OF TRUE LOVE NEVER RUNS SMOOTHLY

— So my grandmother told me when she shared with me the stories of her own life.

Bill and I met at least three times a week for lunch together in the student union cafeteria. We dated nearly every weekend. One day, at lunch, after we'd been seeing each other for several weeks, Bill was pensive. Feeling comfortable with the progress of our relationship, I asked him teasingly what he was thinking. He looked at me very seriously. "I am determined I am going to do well in my studies," he said, "and finish college and have a successful career." I told him approvingly I thought that was an admirable plan.

He then fixed me with a piercing look and said sternly, " — and nothing and nobody is going to keep me from doing that!" My comfort evaporated; a cold chill came over me. But in a short second a hot flame of anger began to kindle in my stomach as I unexpectedly felt rejected. "I think that's very sensible of you," I told him with all the dignity I could muster. "I have no intention, either, of letting anyone get in the way of *my* plan to finish college and work in fascinating foreign countries. Oh! I forgot!" I exclaimed. "I asked my Spanish prof for some extra credit work. I'm supposed to meet him before class, so I have to go right now!" I picked up my books and left, leaving half my sandwich on the table. Bill's expression was an odd combination of relief and dismay. I awaited the start of my Spanish class in a back stairwell, crying quietly by myself.

We had another movie date scheduled for the next evening. My stomach churned, unsure whether Bill would show up. He did, right on time, as usual, but I felt distanced from him. On the way to the movie, Bill asked me. "Do you really intend to work overseas?" "Of course I do," I told him, tartly. "That's what I'm studying for — I want to see the world and meet lots of interesting people. I expect to have a fascinating career!" Bill was very quiet the rest of that evening, but his kiss goodnight was long and lingering.

An unplanned dream had been strongly shouldering aside my original life plan. I had no desire at that point to be anywhere but near Bill. The thought of marriage as a real possibility rather than a "someday-far-in-the-future" idea was beginning to intrude insistently into my thoughts. It was only Bill's aggressive comment about his career plans that made me state so firmly my wavering plan for travel and life overseas. My thoughts were in turmoil.

Bill surprised me by tentatively talking about how different it must be to grow up in a big family. He said he hoped his kids could have that experience rather than being only children like us. Two dreams were definitely competing in my imagination! The first was the original one of foreign travel and the other — if it included Bill — had to do with marriage and a family. It was becoming more and more clear to me the newer dream was not compatible with a career requiring my residence in various overseas posts, even though the idea of seeing the world still appealed to me.

Bill continued to ask, in a variety of ways, if I really intended to work overseas, while his kisses became more lingering and sweet. At first, I continued to tell him that was my plan. But then I began to waver. I conceded I might do that only until "if or when I get married." Bill still looked uncomfortable with my replies, but a little less tense. Variations of that conversation went on through several dates, with my responses gradually indicating I might be losing interest in a career overseas. Bill seemed more and more pleased with my answers to his variously worded queries. His kisses, hugs and caresses were becoming more and more insistent.

But after one unsettling date when our mutual fears were more active than our hopes, we seemed out of synch with each other again. I came home in confusion to cry to myself in bed. Grandma quietly came into my room from hers directly across the hall. She sat on the edge of my bed and waited patiently while I slowly stopped sniffling. "The course of true love never runs smoothly," she reminded me. "Just remember, Dear, always follow your heart. Keep your head on straight when you do it and remain practical and strong. But most of all, stay open to love. That combination of strength and good sense will never lead you astray if you're careful not to let your head dissuade you of what your heart already knows. You can find a way, I'm sure."

Grandma loved two men dearly, was widowed twice by the age of 40, then raised her and their total of five children alone. But she treasured her wonderful memories of love. She left me to think about her words. I decided to be less spiky with Bill. I knew I loved him. I was pretty sure he loved me. I didn't want *any*thing to come between us.

Bill and I continued to see each other as often as we could. When we could not meet, Bill telephoned me every evening. I stopped dating most others, preferring to wait for Bill's calls. All through college, he was a very serious, hard-driving student carrying extra credit hours. He was stern with himself — never letting his life interfere with studying, even if the studying had to run late into the nights. About then, he also managed to squeeze in some part-time work.

Certainly I fell for Bill the first day I met him. Bill appeared to be solidly focused on me from that moment, too, but it took him a little longer to admit it to himself — maybe a few days. We met on Valentine's Day. It wasn't long 'til Bill began talking about the things he hoped for when he married — like a big family. I told him I definitely wanted a big family, amending in my own mind — *'someday.'* "Well, if WE were married," Bill said, in a satisfied way, "that would be a good thing since *our* kids would have no aunts or uncles or cousins."

Bill then skittishly changed the subject. He planned to be a scientist. It was his way to carefully consider all options before coming to any conclusions. He surprised himself by the depth of his feelings for me so early in our relationship. He would have preferred to approach being serious about one girl in a much more logical, step-by-step manner. But his emotions raced ahead of his caution, ignoring his concerns.

By June, Bill began to discuss practical considerations, noting it would be impossible for him to marry anyone — carefully not saying "marry you" — while he was still in college. He declared he would have to finish his studies, become established in a career, and build a bank account. I began to see his slow-to-marry father in him, but I was like a moth to flame. I couldn't resist the emotions bombarding my heart! Bill was so much more important to me that anyone else I had ever dated.

In July, Bill threw caution to the winds and asked me to "go steady." I had been asked before but it had always sounded boring to me to be tied to just one man. Nevertheless, the moment Bill asked me, I surprised myself by responding enthusiastically. "Oh yes, Bill, I'll go steady with you!" "You really WILL?" Bill asked, as if in surprise. "Of course I will!" I said. "That's terrific!" he exclaimed, "I was afraid you'd say no." We were in his mother's car after a date. Despite that awkward gearshift between us, Bill held me close as if he'd never let me go and kissed me passionately. He quietly breathed into my ear, "I'm so glad!" Then he kissed me even more passionately.

Although I stopped dating most others soon after Bill and I met, I continued to see one boy I truly liked as a dear friend. I had been dating him since early in high school. I told Bill I needed to tell Johnny before we could officially go steady. I said I would let him know as soon as I could do that, explaining that it would be unfair to just tell him on the phone that I was "claimed," since I doubted he dated other girls.

A couple of days later, I met Johnny. I braced myself to say I had met someone very special to me, so I couldn't see him anymore. Bill was a man where shy Johnny was a sweet boy, although one with determined strength in him from his lifelong battle with the disability of a lame leg and other ailments caused by polio in early childhood. Despite them, Johnny had managed to become a Civil Air Patrol pilot while still in his teens. He was making plans to teach me to fly, something I would love to have learned. Johnny was quiet for a bit, then collected himself and drew a deep breath. Although his voice was quieter than usual, he thoughtfully wished me well and told me he hoped I would be very happy, noting regretfully, "I guess I won't be able to teach you to fly, after all." He added that he would miss me a lot. We had never even kissed, so I could not throw my arms around him as I wanted to, to tell him I would miss him, too. I felt sad about the end of our friendship, but I knew it meant more to Johnny than it had to me since I met Bill.

Not long before Bill and I were married, I received a call from Johnny's best friend to tell me that Johnny's post-polio problems had claimed his life. He added that Johnny had never dated any other girl but me and always kept my picture on his bedside table. I cried myself to sleep for the courageous boy I had known. I realized then that Johnny occupied a very special place in my heart and would always own that little corner of it. I mourned the affection I had been unable to show him, the unspoken feelings we had been unable to share.

After I forced myself be honest with Johnny, I told Bill, on our next date, that I was free to go steady with him. His kiss was quick and ardent. "I was so worried you'd change your mind!" he told me, holding me so tightly I could barely breathe.

THE SURPRISING BIRTHDAY GIFT

In August, I wondered if Bill would remember it was my birthday. I had a full-time summer job to save for tuition, but I asked for that day off to be available for anything Bill might want to do. By early afternoon, having heard nothing from him since his phone call the night before, I sat down in the living room to try to read.

Hearing a commotion outside, I looked out the window. Bill and a friend from college were at the back of the truck the other man drove to school each day, pulling out … something. I saw it was a cedar chest! Racing into the kitchen, I told Mother, adding, "Mum! What will I do? What should I say?" reiterating, "He's bringing in a *cedar chest*!" Mother turned from the sink, put her wet hands on her hips, looked at me piercingly, said, "It's obvious he can't quite manage to say what he wants to. But a cedar chest clearly indicates his meaning. You know how you feel, so simply accept it prettily, thank him, and kiss him soundly. Then you can shake the other fellow's hand and thank him for helping."

I was almost as astonished at her calm response as I was at the idea of Bill's carting a cedar chest up our walk! I turned and ran to answer the doorbell and exclaim as if I had not seen it arriving. "What's THIS?" "It's a birthday present for you, " Bill said somewhat breathlessly as he and the other man turned the chest on it's side to carefully ease it through the doorway. "Where can we put it down?" Mother appeared behind me, saying calmly, "I think it would fit nicely in the front dining room window." I turned in surprise to see that while I was answering the door, Mum had moved her favorite houseplant to the side window to make room. The two men carefully carried the chest into the dining room.

I did exactly as Mother advised. I threw my arms around Bill and kissed him "soundly." Without a pause, I then turned and reached for our schoolmate's hand to thank him for helping to move it in. Bill began to grin like a little boy with a very large lollipop. He said, "We have to hurry back so Rick and I can get to our next classes, but I'll be back later!" Mum injected, "Will you come back then for dinner, Bill? I'm making meat loaf." "Yes, thank you," he answered as he hurried out the door. "Six o'clock," Mum called to him as he left.

After they drove away, I sat down on a dining room chair to admire the beautiful new cedar chest. I hoped it meant to Bill what it traditionally did, but in the absence of any sort of declaration from him, I wasn't sure. "Well, aren't you going to open it and look inside?" Mum called from the kitchen. "Oh! Yes! I guess I should." I found a shiny new penny in it! I was surprised that Bill knew the tradition of putting a new coin in a box given as a gift — for good luck and long life. I certainly hoped that meant a long life together. That was the sort of good luck I wanted most of all!

When Bill came back, I wore a dress instead of my knock-around-the-house slacks. Bill was tidied up, too, in a fresh shirt. He brought me a very sentimental birthday card — the first of many, many sentimental cards over our lifetime together. I read it and looked up at him with eyes brimming. He said, " — And I mean every word." Time after time, for the rest of our lives together, whenever Bill gave me a carefully chosen card, which said what he could not put into his own words, he repeated that thought.

Mother suggested Dad take pictures of us with the new cedar chest. Although Bill was basically a very serious-minded man, he always found a lot to smile about. It was that smile that first captured my attention. Over sixty years later, only two or three of my many photos of Bill lack his trademark smile. The cedar chest photos are without it. Wordlessly, he had just taken a long step into his future.

After dinner, we went out, supposedly to have a soda at the drugstore, but instead we parked a couple of blocks away in front of a vacant building site. We kissed and hugged and talked inanely of almost anything *other* than the cedar chest and its traditional meaning as a place for a bride-to-be to collect linens and blankets for her future home.

A NEW DATE DRESS

We continued to date as often as we could, except nights when Bill had to study for an important class or exam, but nothing of marriage was voiced except in terms of "if we were to marry, then …" Beneath the surface, we both knew where we wanted to be, but Bill wasn't quite sure how to get there or when to jump off that cliff to make an irrevocable commitment. After the cedar chest gift, my girlfriends kept quizzing me about when we planned to marry, but I could not relieve their curiosity since Bill never spoke of it. The next school year began with a large question mark still in my mind.

I knew what I wanted and that was a life with Bill. But with so little input from him, I was unsure what he was thinking. My planned career hovered in my thoughts as a less-than-ideal fallback idea. I considered taking a semester off school to work and save money, but mostly to give myself time to think about my future. I decided to wait till the end of the Fall semester to make a decision about that, and continued to slog through my classes. But my studies no longer had my full attention. A large portion of my thoughts were reserved for Bill.

One evening, Bill spoke questioningly about ways "people" could afford to marry while in college on the G.I. Bill. I discussed how to stretch dollars, how wives could contribute. Another evening after several such conversations had skirted that specific issue, Bill declared, "MY wife will never have to work! If I couldn't support her, I would have no self-respect!" I told him his ideas were too old-fashioned, still locked in an era when women were denied education. "Would you want a silly, simpering wife whose world is no larger than her home, who could not talk to you intelligently?" I asked him, adding indignantly, " — In which case, you'd better shop for her someplace other than a *college!* IS that the sort of woman you'd marry?" "Of course not!" he replied. "Then why," I asked, " would you want to imprison an intelligent woman in childlike dependency, refusing to allow her to use her good sense to contribute to a partnership?" The thought was obviously a new one to him. He answered honestly. "I don't know."

We were sitting in front of my house in his mother's car. To Bill's surprise, I threw my arms around him, kissed him passionately, then said rather primly, "Well, perhaps you should think about it, then!" I stepped out of the car, quickly strode up the walk, waved to him, then went inside, closing the door firmly behind me. Ignoring Mother's curious look, I went directly upstairs and closed my bedroom door. I did not sleep peacefully that night. My emotions were a-boil between wanting nothing more than to please Bill and my own innate sense of independence.

Mother was aware that Bill had not walked me to the door as usual. In the morning, she told me, somewhat questioningly, that Bill had remained parked outside the house for several minutes before he drove away. "Did he?" I said. "I wonder why?"

I was unaware that, in early October, Bill asked Mother's help in a project. He wanted her to filch from my room one of the various colored glass rings I wore. I bought them at the Five-and-Dime just for their color, each one to match an outfit. Bill had noticed. Mother did as Bill asked. When I complained that I couldn't find the ring to match a specific outfit, she said, "Well, you must have left it somewhere — perhaps in a pocket or a handbag." I gave up and changed to another outfit.

I was also unaware that Bill returned the borrowed ring to Mother and spoke at length to my parents while I was at a sorority meeting. When I came home, Mother asked me, "Didn't you say you and Bill are going dancing next Saturday?" "Yes, that's right." "Well, don't you think your date dresses are beginning to look somewhat shabby? I think you ought to buy another one or two — one, at least."

"Oh, Mother, you know I'm saving my money. I don't need another date dress." "Yes, you *do*!" Mother insisted. "Why don't we go shopping together Friday evening? The stores will all be open." I was amazed. With Mother's high blood pressure and fallen arches, she usually intensely disliked shopping! "Mother, you hate shopping!" I protested. "Only when I have to buy things for myself. I *love* to shop with other people!" she declared firmly. I was so surprised I agreed to a shopping trip that Friday to buy an inexpensive dress — one that would "do."

Mother gravitated toward the higher-priced racks, bringing back to the fitting room a beautiful blue dress with a jewel neckline, long sleeves and a flirty peplum. I looked at the price tag and pushed it away as if it were hot. "Mother! It's beautiful, but did you *look* at that price tag? It costs 18 dollars!!" "Yes, I did. You have enough saved, and you'll be saving more as you go on. You can spend a little extra something on yourself *once* in a while! You're beginning to look shabby. You embarrass me!" Despite the fact that she pinched pennies till they screamed to help as many other people as possible throughout the Great Depression, Mother was always careful never to look "ragtag."

I really did love the color of the dress. I gave in and tried it on. It fit perfectly — sleekly fitted unlike most of my fuller-skirted dresses — and it made my eyes appear a deeper blue than they really were. I walked out with a dress box in hand, still amazed at Mother — and at myself for giving in when I had pledged myself to thrift.

The next morning, Mother said, "Now, this is the evening you and Bill are going out to that Chestnut Lodge place to dance, isn't it? You *are* going to wear your nice new dress, aren't you?" "I suppose that's as good a place as any to wear it for the first time," I responded, "but maybe I ought to save it for more of a special occasion."

"NO!" Mother insisted vehemently. "It's a very pretty dress and you look quite nice in it. You ought to wear it. Bill will love the way you look!" Oh, well. She seemed so determined that I gave in. "OK, I guess I'll wear it tonight." And I did.

THE NOT-QUITE-PROPOSAL

Bill never did quite manage to propose to me. Instead, he reached for my left hand immediately after he turned off the engine in the parking lot at the Chestnut Lodge, and held it up to the light of the street lamp out at the curb. Then he slipped a ring onto it — a *diamond* ring. It fit perfectly. Astonished, not sure I was seeing what I thought it was, I turned my hand toward the light. It *was* a diamond ring!

"Will you wear it?" Bill asked, very seriously. All my internal quibbling about the distance between independence and loving Bill melded into one quick, heartfelt response, "Oh yes, Bill. Of COURSE I will, Darling!" I threw my arms around him and heard him whisper — to himself, I think — as if he'd been holding his breath, "Wo-o-ow! I just won the biggest bet in the whole wide world!" Then, in the semi-light from the street lamp, he looked into my eyes and said, "I don't know what I would have done if you hadn't said yes. I love you s-o-o much!"

Suddenly I thought about Mother insisting I have a new dress for that evening. "Did my parents know about this?" I asked. "Yes, of course," Bill replied, in his most serious tone of voice. "I had to have their permission to ask you to marry me." "Bill Keeber, you did NOT ask me to marry you! First you gave me a cedar chest without saying a word about marriage, and then you simply put a ring on my finger!" "Of course I asked you," he said with insistent logic. "I asked if you'd wear it." His voice shook a little, "— I wasn't sure you would." Then he added elatedly, his voice a bit husky, "But you *said* you would." He added as if to himself. "You *really* said you *would!*" He kissed me firmly, as if emphasizing the point. "'C'mon!" he grinned at me. "I want to buy us a bottle of champagne!"

We went into the Chestnut Lodge where we'd gone dancing so many times and knew all the staff. Bill ordered champagne from the smiling waiter as I turned my hand to admire the diamond in the light from the candle on the table. "A celebration, I assume," the waiter said. Wordlessly, Bill reached for my hand and held it up. The waiter nodded and left.

The champagne arrived — *with* the owner and the entire wait staff. "THIS is on the house!" the owner said. He lifted the bottle high, turning to the band and other patrons, "*Congratulations* to our two sweethearts!" One of the waitresses pounced on me to give me a warm hug. The others all followed suit. The waiters wrung Bill's hand. The owner stood beaming.

Just then, the band struck up our favorite tune, "Begin the Beguine." The owner leaned over, popped the cork, poured two glassfuls and gestured to us to drink. We sipped, then Bill tilted his glass toward me in a salutary manner. His eyes holding mine, he placed the glass carefully on the table, stood up and held out his hand.

Putting down my own glass, I rose and together we moved onto the dance floor to our favorite music. The roving spotlight found us and stayed with us. Other dancers moved off the floor to stand at the sides clapping. We had expected a quiet celebration between the two of us, but our engagement evening couldn't have been more romantic. After the dance, we went back to our table where the owner had whisked away the two partly consumed glasses and brought out fresh ones so he could again pour us our bubbly with a flourish. "*Lifelong happiness* to our lovers!" he exclaimed loudly. We beamed, he beamed, other patrons smiled, clapped, and came over to hug me and shake Bill's hand. It was so much more of a special occasion than we ever expected.

I thought of the dress I was wearing and silently blessed Mother for insisting I buy it. I kept that dress for years and years and wore it often, always thrilled by the look of admiration in Bill's eyes. Eventually it wore out and I carefully folded it up and put it into the cedar chest until children's woolies displaced it one summer. I have regretted discarding it ever since. I would so love to see that beautiful color again.

THE GREEN-EYED MONSTER

After we were engaged, Bill and I both worked hard to save money so we could afford to marry. Bill and I knew only one of us could afford college after we married, so I decided not to return to school. I notified my counselor so my scholarship could be re-awarded. Bill promised me solemnly that after he had his degree, was working and we could afford it, he would pay the tuition for me to return to school for my own degree.

One afternoon, shortly after our engagement, thinking of the overtime to add to our "marriage fund," I gladly agreed to work late on a project my engineer boss was trying to complete on time. Bill called me at the office to remind me tersely that we had a date that evening. He was calling from my house, having arrived to pick me up for a movie. It was the first time I had ever forgotten a date with him but, deep into maps and paperwork, I had not noticed the time.

I told him I'd had to work late, but he could pick me up at work. He did, but was stiff and unresponsive as I told him enthusiastically of my boss's project and how much we accomplished. Bill drove me directly home, since I suggested it was too late for the movie, so we could dance to the old Victrola in the basement instead. Bill nodded, but said almost nothing on the trip home.

When he pulled up at my parents' house, Bill reached over and took my hand. Holding it tightly, almost painfully tightly, he looked at me very intently and asked, "Are you interested in that engineer?" "What engineer?" I asked, astonished. "Your boss," Bill said. "What a silly idea!" I scoffed, about to add that my boss was newly married and happily so. But before I could go on, Bill dropped my hand to thump his fist on the steering wheel. He said, "I really *hate* to have you working in that office with all those engineer types day after day!"

I was astonished! Thoughts of the various engineers at the telephone company where I worked flashed through my mind — Mr. Jakes, 50-ish, continually worried about his teen-age kids — overweight Donald Masterson, in his mid-40's, with pictures of his blowsy girlfriend prominently displayed on his desk — two men old enough to be counting the days to retirement — and my boss, a handsome blue-eyed, dark-haired Irishman of considerable charm, whom all the girls on the staff admired from afar the way one does a movie star who will never be "available." He was madly in love with his new wife and talking enthusiastically about the family they wanted. He was a thoroughly likeable man, but I never thought of him romantically. I was happily committed to Bill.

I began to simmer and rapidly reached a near-boil. My mind turned to a pale, pretty neighbor, effectively imprisoned in her home down the block. She didn't dare walk alone with their little girl in the carriage for fear of her husband's insanely imaginative jealousy and hot temper. Turning to Bill, I said, "Your jealousy does neither of us any compliment. If you don't trust me to be true when I'm promised to you, then I'm not the wife for you. Jealously would tear us apart. I will not live with a man who imagines all sorts of improbabilities!"

With that, I removed my engagement ring and placed it in Bill's hand. "Go home and think about your jealousy. If you believe you can overcome it, you may come back in two weeks and offer me that ring again. If not, don't come back at all." Disregarding Bill's look of hurt astonishment, I dashed into the house past my surprised parents, trying to hold back tears till I reached my room.

The doorbell rang downstairs. Mother called up the stairs. "Bea, Bill wants to speak to you." "Tell him I'll talk to him in two weeks and not a minute sooner." I buried my head in my pillow so she couldn't hear me crying. I heard further conversation downstairs, then Mother called upstairs again. "Bea, Bill says he MUST speak to you." I didn't reply. Instead, I went to my door and closed it with a snap.

After more conversation downstairs, with my father's very reasonable voice joining in the mix, I heard the front door close and the sound of Bill's mother's car receding as it moved down the street away from me.

Grandma came into my room. Having overheard the conversation between Mother, Dad and Bill, she patted me sympathetically on the back and told me, "You did the right thing, Dear. Jealousy is the most corrosive emotion in the world. I once sent Francis away with my engagement ring for the very same reason. Mother was furious with me for risking a good marriage, but I wouldn't relent. Francis soon came back, ring in hand, to tell me he would never speak of jealousy again. And he did not. Be strong, Dear. I'm sure Bill will make the right decision." Not half as sure as Grandma, I burst into fresh tears. She patted my back, told me to have faith in my true love, and left me with my fears and second thoughts.

The next morning, as I was leaving for work, the telephone rang. Mother answered it. "Bea, Bill would like to speak to you." "Please tell him I'll talk to him in two weeks if he still wishes me to," I said, and headed out the door to catch the bus for downtown. My boss noticed the lack of my ring (and probably also my puffy eyes) and asked about it. I told him it was in for repairs.

Bill called every morning and every evening. Mother became quite cross with me. I stood my ground, even though tears were always near the surface when I refused to take Bill's calls and often in between.

Finally, the morning of the 13th day, a Thursday, Bill rang the doorbell a few seconds before 7 a.m.

Mother, still in her robe, invited him in. I had just finished dressing for work. She called me to come downstairs, adding, "Quickly!" I did, wondering what she wanted so urgently. As I stepped off the bottom step into the hall, I was astonished to see Mother disappear into her bedroom, followed by the click of the latch. I overheard heard quick, quiet words between Mother and Dad. Their bedroom door opened a crack, then Mother said, more clearly, "No, John, this is between *them*!" Their door closed again firmly.

It was at that moment I saw Bill standing in the doorway. He held out the ring. I walked slowly toward him, the sight of him completely driving out of my memory my determination not to speak to him till 14 days after I returned his ring. "Bea, PLEASE put this back on your finger." Tears sprang to my eyes. "Come!" I said, "out to the car!"

I ran past Bill, grabbed a coat from the front hall closet, and hurried toward his mother's car at the curb, where I dove into the passenger door. He followed me, slid into the driver's side, then turned to me. Unable to speak, I motioned for him to start the engine and move on down the street. He pulled into the end of a nearby street in a subdivision where construction had not yet started. Stamping on the brake, he turned and held the ring out toward me in his open palm. He asked, almost angrily, but with an underlying note of pleading in his voice, "Bea, WILL you take this back?" adding hesitantly, " … or … not?"

I leaned away from him. "You haven't said what I need to he-e-ear!" It was half a wail, half a challenge. He looked at me for a long, silent moment, then said quietly, "You're right. I haven't. I did think about it — a lot. It was dishonorable of me not to trust you. I know you are true or you would have told me in advance before taking up with somebody else just the way you told that Johnny before you started going steady with me. I promise never to be jealous again." He took a deep breath, then said, "PLEASE take back this ring, Bea. Please — take *me* back."

Huddling on the far side of my seat, I whispered, "Oh Bill, I love you so. I was so afraid you wouldn't come back!" "How could you *think* that? I called and called and you kept refusing to talk to me. I heard your mother call you. I heard you refuse every time. How could you *possibly* think I wouldn't come back?" "I wasn't sure you'd come back without promising never to be jealous again!" "I do promise! I'll never doubt you again, Bea. Please take me back." I could see he meant it.

Not trusting myself to say anything more, I stretched out my right hand, palm up. But Bill took my other hand to solemnly slip the ring onto my fourth finger as he had done the night he first gave it to me. We reached for each other past that abominable gearshift. My tears soaked the front of Bill's jacket. Then I felt moisture behind my ear. I looked up to see Bill trying shakily to smile at me with shimmering tears in his eyes. He said, "I was so afraid I had really lost you. If you hadn't taken me back, the whole rest of my life would have been worthless!" "I know. Me, too!" I answered. "I kept wondering if I was wrong. I didn't want to lose you, but I'm so afraid of jealousy. I was afraid it would destroy us. I'll never be jealous of you, either, Bill. I promise! I know you'll be true."

We stayed in each other's arms for a long moment more. Then I remembered the time. "Oh!" I said, "I'll be late for work! … But how can I go in looking like this, with my eyes all red and puffy from crying?" "You can't possibly." Bill smiled at me with a very satisfied look. "Let's go back to your house and ask your mother to call in an excuse for you. I'm going to cut ALL my classes today and we're going to spend the whole day figuring out how — and how <u>soon</u> — we can manage to get married. It's time to stop waiting for the ideal money situation. We'll just *have* to figure this out." Then, perhaps because Bill was so innately a scientist who had to methodically work through every step of a problem before coming to a conclusion, he added, "There *has* to be a way we can be together somehow. It's only logical."

Mother called to tell my boss I was ill and would not be back 'til Monday. Bill and I did just as we both wanted. We drove out to my aunt and uncle's cottage where we could park and talk undisturbed, and hug and kiss in between. We discussed how we could marry on the G. I. Bill. We agreed we still needed some time to save for household necessities, but then went to tell my parents we had set a date — June, 1948 — two years and four months from when we met. With Dad's and Bill's math skills, they determined which dates that month and year would be a Saturday and we chose the 12th. For the next 60-plus years, I never doubted Bill's fidelity and he never again questioned mine.

I FOUND US AN APARTMENT!

About two months before our wedding, Bill called me. "I found us an apartment!" he told me excitedly. Apartments, after World War II, with so many veterans returning home and marrying, were scarce as hens' teeth. But Bill managed to find one for us and rented it on the spot, giving us time to fix it up. It needed it, but we felt very fortunate to have a place of our own to begin married life, instead of having to return to my parents' house from our honeymoon.

Ours was the center one of three apartments above stores in a very old building, at the corner just three doors from Bill's parents' house. Bill and I, with my father's and Bill's mom's help, cleaned it up with hot water, soap, paint, wallpaper, elbow grease and sweat. It was where Bill and I first made intimate love a week before our wedding.

A friend and his truck were available that Sunday to help move in our furniture. The brand-new stove and refrigerator we chose together had been installed a few days earlier. Only the wallpapering in our bedroom was not yet finished. The two men collected furniture from Bill's and my parents' houses and put it all in place in the apartment. But there was no place for our bedroom furniture.

Our two bedroom dressers were crammed into the dinette and kitchen between the furnishings and appliances already there. Spreading a painter's drop cloth on the tiny second bedroom floor, we stored our new double mattress there, bordered on three sides with stacked boxes of wedding gifts. Nothing more would fit into that little room. Our bedspring and the head and footboards were stacked between couch and chairs. There was no room left for us to walk through the living room. To reach the second bedroom, I had to climb over the arm of the couch, crawl on hands and knees across it, then over the other arm.

When our friend left with his truck, Bill was achy and tired. We decided to lock the apartment to go rustle up a belated lunch, but I couldn't budge the open sash in the small bedroom. I called Bill. He climbed over the couch to come help. That new mattress beckoned him. Stretching out on it, Bill commented, "Oh, this feels so-o go-o-o-od. I found muscles I didn't know I had, carrying that furniture up those stairs!" I kneeled beside him to massage his back. Bill groaned with the relief it gave him, then turned over and playfully pulled me down into his arms. I laughed, then Bill kissed me quiet. Surprising myself and perhaps Bill, too, I responded with all the pent-up longing of the last months. Breathlessly, Bill fumbled to unbutton my blouse. Reflexively, I raised my hand to stop him, but never touched his as he kissed my ear, my neck, then moved down into my cleavage. Moved solely by our mutual desire, we forgot all our intentions of "waiting till after the wedding." Quickly removing our restraining clothing, we made passionate love. We finally lay still, side by side on the bare new mattress. Then Bill leaned up on his elbow, looked into my eyes and told me quietly, "I don't think you can possibly imagine how much I love you." I put my arms around his neck, pulled his head down to kiss his lips — and we made love again. Afterwards, I recalled, "I don't know the time, but your parents are expecting us for dinner, you know."

Bill checked his watch. "Oops! We'd better get moving or Mom might come running down the street to tell us dinner's getting cold!" We hurried into our clothes and locked up the apartment. I'm sure I was flushed. Bill certainly looked happy.

"Well, I c'n see you both look ver' pleased," his father said with the slurs in his speech he had suffered since his stroke. "Is 't all 'n order?" "No," Bill told him. "It looked pretty nice till we moved in those last bedroom pieces. Now we can barely move around everything." Just then, his mother called out, "Dinner's ready! Hurry up and help Dad to the table." So we did just that.

On Monday morning, my boss greeted me as I arrived at work. Comparatively newly married, he was an unabashed romantic. "My!" he said, "Anticipation of next Saturday is making you positively rosy." He added chivalrously, "It's making you even prettier than usual. I hope your fiancé appreciates that!" I knew it wasn't anticipation but the previous afternoon that produced the persistent glow, so I just smiled.

The next three evenings, we worked on completing the work in the apartment. Finally, the bedroom was finished and we moved everything into that room late Wednesday evening, leaving the spare bedroom to the remaining boxes of wedding gifts. By then, it was nearly 10 p.m. and our alarms would awaken us early the next morning for work and school. On Thursday, I had to hurry from work to the bridal shop for my gown. Friday evening was the wedding rehearsal. There was never a chance to make use of that mattress again before the wedding on Saturday.

THE FORGOTTEN WEDDING

It's not that the wedding didn't take place. It certainly did. We have an album of pictures to prove it.

The night before it was more in question. After the wedding rehearsal, Mother asserted her final parental authority by insisting I come home to bed for a good sleep rather than going out with Bill and the wedding party. I lay in bed, wide awake, becoming rapidly more nervous. Where my concerns came from, I can't imagine! Doubts grew, fears ran rampant in my mind. I was too young, I told myself. I didn't know how to cook. I had never done housework, Mother impatient with my fumbling efforts. I had never done laundry — had never even washed out a pair of my own stockings! How could I possibly marry and permit Bill to see all my disastrous deficits of experience and skill? What if he divorced me because of them? I climbed out of bed, put on my slippers and robe and marched downstairs to the living room. Mum was already asleep but Dad was still sitting up reading.

"This is a terrible mistake! I am nowhere near ready to get married!" I burst out to Dad, tears streaming down my face. "I can't go through with this!" Dad looked up at me, laid his book aside to give me his full attention, then said, calmly and quietly, "Well, if you're not sure, of course it would be best to call it off." Relieved, I nodded, my heart pounding. Then Dad went on, "It's too late now to call the invited guests. Why don't you just go back to bed and have a good sleep so we can take care of all that tomorrow?" Calmed, I told Dad I loved him, then — relieved of worry — marched back to my room to sleep.

I recall the day of the wedding, too. Grandma came into my bedroom to say brightly, "Wake up, Sleepyhead! You can't dream the whole day away. We've made you a special breakfast." With no further thought, I went downstairs to find an elegant repast served on Mother's best china. As we finished the last of it, Mother said, "You'll have to hurry. Your Aunt Evelyn will be here in a few minutes to do your nails." Obediently I hurried upstairs and finished dressing just as the doorbell rang.

After my nails were dry, I wrote a few more wedding gift thank you notes. Mother and Aunt Evelyn chatted in the kitchen until Mother announced, "Lunch is ready, everyone. Evy brought a beautiful chicken salad for us to enjoy."

In the afternoon, Aunt Elsie arrived to do my hair. The anticipation and excitement were building. I tried reading, Dad's method for remaining calm. It didn't work, so I decided to write a few more notes.

Dad walked into the dining room and stood beside me. I looked up at him. "When do you want to start calling the guests to tell them the wedding is off?" he asked mildly. My mouth must have formed a perfect "o" as I recalled the previous night's pre-wedding jitters. "Oh Dad! I can't call off the wedding! It would break Bill's heart, and anyway, I WANT to get married!" With a twinkle in his eye, Dad said, "It was just nerves. I knew you weren't really going to call it off. But you were too overwrought last night for me to reason with you." He patted my shoulder and returned to his book. My cheeks felt hot as I turned back to my note cards.

After an early dinner, Alice, my matron of honor, and Joanne, my bridesmaid, arrived with their gowns in garment bags, to dress and help me dress. My bedroom was a flurry of underwear, stockings, petticoats and giggles. Mother called upstairs just as Alice dropped my wedding gown over my head with Joanne carefully holding a large paper bag over my hairdo so it wouldn't rumple. The photographer had arrived.

We girls went downstairs to meet Milt, a college friend who had offered to do our photos and album as his and his wife's wedding gift to us. We all posed while Milt shot one picture after another. Mother and Grandma left for the church with my cousin Jack, one of the groomsmen. Charles, the other groomsman, a childhood friend of Bill's, whisked Alice and Joanne away. A neighbor, Mr. Snyder, who had volunteered his brand new Cadillac, pulled up in front of the house right on schedule for Dad and me. Milt snapped a couple more pictures, then left in his car to race to the church to be there in advance of our arrival.

Mr. Snyder drove us around the block a couple of times, to stop at St. Clement's Episcopal Church at exactly five minutes to seven to face Milt's flashbulbs as we alighted from the car. Dad hustled me into the church where Alice and Joanne waited. Mum tweaked my veil, then allowed Jack to escort her down the aisle while my eldest cousin, Betty, the church organist, played. Joanne, then Alice, took their turns walking down the aisle. I peeked past them to see Bill emerge from the choir room with Bob, his best man. Betty struck up the Wedding March and Dad took my arm. "Ready?" he asked me huskily. I nodded. As we walked slowly to Betty's music, my ears noted some "oohs" and "ahhs," Bill's dad sniffling emotionally, unable to control his feelings, his mother's insistent "Sh-h! Sh-h-h!"

But I saw nothing except Bill's beautiful maple syrup eyes all the way down the aisle.

And that's all I recall. I know nothing past that. I don't recall the priest's words, the wedding vows we promised. I only recall Bill's warm eyes full of love and admiration. The organ began again triumphantly. I heard the priest say, "You may now kiss your bride!" and Bill did. It wasn't a formal, dry peck. It was a real kiss that promised so much!

We turned and I felt a moment's surprise to see all those smiling people — Bill's and my parents, cousins, aunts, uncles, friends and neighbors. I really tried to look dignified. I didn't succeed. Aunt Elsie later said I walked down the aisle on Bill's arm looking "as pleased as the cat that ate the canary!" Aunt Evelyn put us all in order for the receiving line. I smiled at Bill, who was grinning elatedly.

Mum turned to us and said, "Dad and I would like you both to come home to visit often. And Bea, come home anytime you want, even when Bill's too busy. But never, ever come home to us after a fight with your husband. Always work out disagreements together." She kissed me, then Bill. I sobered momentarily, Mum's words driving home to me that my future lay irrevocably with the man beside me. And I was equally committed to his. Then I looked into Bill's eyes and knew that was a wonderful idea. The guests began to file past. Milt's flashbulbs blinded us momentarily each time he took another photo.

Mr. Snyder sedately drove us around the block to the church hall steps, where we alighted and started to dash in to our wedding reception. A light rain had begun to fall, so we hurried to the door. My shoe skidded on the moist step, but I didn't fall. Bill held my arm firmly, keeping me safe.

At the reception, Bill's cousin Jerry, there from New York for the occasion, was to offer the toast. But first, he told the gathered family and friends that he and Bill's parents were ready and waiting for Bill to drive to the church together. Bill appeared in the living room wearing his shirt and tie under his bathrobe, asking icily, "OK, who's the joker who hid my pants?" "You mean, those slacks over your left arm?" asked Jerry.

Looking at them in surprise, Bill retreated up the stairs to finish dressing. As the wedding guests chuckled, I was relieved to know I wasn't the only one with pre-wedding jitters.

Later, Alice and Joanne helped me change into my traveling outfit in a Sunday school room. Alice, Bill and I hurried to Bob's car, waiting at the curb to drive us to the Statler Hotel. At Bill's insistence, Bob's car bore none of the traditional ribbons, chalked lettering or tied-on cans to rattle and bounce noisily behind us. Bill worked at the hotel as a bellhop during high school so he knew his way around the registration process. Determined no smirking desk clerks would know we were newly married, he arranged for me to give him my suitcase at the wedding rehearsal. In the afternoon before the wedding, he checked in and took our cases to the room. He planned a dignified arrival with no fuss and feathers.

Despite driving quite sedately, Bob kept taking wrong turns, getting lost. I couldn't understand it; Bob was a Buffalo native and the Statler was a long-time fixture of the city. He said he was nervous, never having been a "Best Man" before. Eventually, he found his way and pulled up at the front entry. As Bill stepped out and reached for my hand, Bob and Alice turned to say, "Have a happy honeymoon, guys!" Bob gunned the engine as we turned to enter the large double doors held open by the bowing doorman.

We walked in unhurriedly. I stood back studying the lobby décor while Bill stepped to the desk to say firmly, "Key, please — Keeber." An unsmiling clerk handed it to him. Dignity intact, Bill took my arm to head toward the elevator. Just then, we saw Bob and Alice breathlessly rushing through the door. Astonished, we turned toward them just as the entire wedding party jumped from behind pillars and furniture, yelling, "Happy honeymoon!" "Newlyweds! Newlyweds!" The desk clerk grinned, other guests turned to smile, and one well-oiled man emerging from the bar wordlessly thumped Bill's back. Bill gave up all hope of a quiet entrance. We followed our friends into the hotel bar for a drink. After a few minutes, we quietly left them there celebrating our wedding while we escaped to the elevator unnoticed.

To this day, I can't recall the wedding ceremony. I know I agreed to love, honor and cherish. I know I said, "I do." I know Bill agreed to all that, too. He *told* me I did, and he did, and I believed him. Somehow, magically, I found on my hand a wedding ring, which hadn't been there when I entered the church. And one was on Bill's hand, too, which I knew I had given to Alice to carry down the aisle to keep until I was called upon to put it on Bill's finger. So I'm sure we were married right and proper. But I have no recollection of anything between my sight of Bill's eyes awaiting me at the front of the church and the moment we kissed and turned to walk back down the aisle together — married.

HONEYMOON DAZED

Our trip to New York City was my first train ride. Bill competently turned our bags over to a porter, found our car, gallantly took my arm to help me aboard. He found our seats with as much confidence as if he'd been working on that train. Traveling east, I was fascinated by the sights, my head swiveling so I wouldn't miss a thing. We enjoyed an elegant lunch in the dining car, our waiter smilingly, quietly efficient and attentive. Bill seemed to take it all in stride, while I was truly a small-town girl exposed for the first time to a life I had only glimpsed in magazines and movies! I was so impressed with Bill's easy sophistication!

In New York, with efficient aplomb, Bill gathered our luggage, hailed a taxi, gave the driver the address of our hotel near Times Square. We dined that first night in the city at elegant Emil's on 49th Street, them wandered around Times Square. The lights, flashing signs and frenetic activity amazed me! Bill was delighted to show me around, recalling the Square from his youthful travels to visit family.

That week, in addition to the luxury of appreciating one another's company for an entire week without other claims on our time, we saw some of the famous sights of New York — the Automat, Rockefeller Center with lunch at its International Restaurant, an art gallery, the Statue of Liberty, Bronx Zoo, Empire State Building, saw a performance by the Rockettes and the Broadway play, "Look, Ma! I'm Dancin'!"

Experiencing famous and varied dining spots — The Headquarters, Ruby Foo's Chinese, Mama Leoni's Italian, and Luchow's German restaurants — was a revelation to me. After my mother's unremarkable cooking, despite acquaintance with Bill's mom's excellent fare, it amazed me that gourmet food could taste so wonderful! My eyes were opened to the whole new world of epicurean dining. It inspired me to want to learn to cook well.

The memory from our honeymoon that I hold closest to my heart, in addition to having my first glimpse of the capable world traveler my husband would someday become, and that it was the start of a wonderful, lengthy marriage, was Bill's wondering comment that first night at our hotel in New York after we experienced the crowds in Times Square: "I just can't get over how lucky we were to find each other out of all the other people in the world!" I know there was no other man who would have been as good a husband for me, and Bill was equally convinced he could never find another woman to so well partner with him for life. I can't begin to remember how many times Bill repeated that thought in the following years. Even now, I keep wondering how — when I was so young and new at adult life! — I was so fortunate to meet Bill and know immediately he was the right man for me.

After a whirlwind week, we returned to Buffalo on Saturday, June 19th, to our own ready-and-waiting apartment in old Cold Spring.

COLD SPRING

— was the name of the neighborhood where Bill grew up.

Between the upper Great Lakes and Niagara Falls, Buffalo had been a shipping, railroad and industrial center for years. "Lakes" freighters off-loaded cargoes there for the city's factories or further shipment by rail. With its docks, railways, and manufacturing plants, Buffalo provided employment for workers of many backgrounds. And nearby Lackawanna's heavy steel industry provided well-paid livings to generations of immigrant workers.

The city had long been composed of individual neighborhoods to which were drawn workers of specific nationalities, faiths and colors. Although each such identifiable neighborhood had "other" families living in them, the majority of people living in close proximity were of the same background. Bill grew up in the 1930's in Cold Spring, Buffalo's traditional German neighborhood. It was only about two-and-a-half years after the end of World War II when we moved into our apartment there.

Cold Spring boasted many turn-of-the-century double- and triple-floor houses along with more modest ones. Bill's parents' home was one of the larger ones. Mom K took in roomers to occupy the second-floor bedrooms. Bill's bedroom and the attic were on the third floor. Predominantly German and white, Cold Spring struggled valiantly to remain middle-class throughout the hard years of the Great Depression.

With the start of World War II, the city's factories geared up for war production. After the lean years of Depression unemployment, people flocked to Buffalo in droves seeking the jobs which proliferated. After wartime prosperity padded their savings, many city families moved to newer suburban homes, leaving less-costly city houses for sale or rent to new arrivals of many backgrounds. Occupying what became available they did not necessarily move into "their own" traditional ethnic neighborhoods.

When Bill and I married, Cold Spring was still a blue-collar middle-class neighborhood composed of the remaining German families and an increasing number of newly-arrived workers from varied backgrounds. The needs of Buffalo's factories for war workers had started a migration. When production returned to peacetime products — utilized in greater and greater numbers by returning veterans and their rapidly growing families — that migration continued and expanded. Change in Cold Spring speeded up, as it did in the rest of the city.

Soon after our marriage, the city cleared out a near-downtown area for "urban development" — claiming houses for unpaid taxes, condemning others in poor repair to raze them, evicting residents, mostly black families whose poorly-educated wage earners garnered incomes barely sufficient to meet current bills. Twos and threes of those families pooled their resources to rent city dwellings together. During the seven years we lived there, Cold Spring became progressively more economically and racially mixed, and considerably more populous than Bill had ever seen it.

HONKY-TONK HYMNS

"Omigod! WHAT is that *noise*?" Bill sat straight up in bed, awakened from a deep sleep. It was 8:00 a.m. plus about one second on Sunday morning. We returned from our honeymoon late the evening before and planned to sleep late. I sat up, too. Listening for a moment, I thought I recognized a hymn, although it certainly didn't sound like anything my cousin Betty ever played in church. First of all, it was extremely loud. Then it had a catchy beat that sounded more like something that might emanate from the open door of a very full, very active dance bar — honky-tonk, no question about it!

I considered it for a few breaths and told Bill, "It's coming from the apartment next door. It does sound *sort* of like a hymn — I *think* it's a hymn, but I'm not sure." Looking thoroughly out of sorts, Bill snorted and lay back down with a thump, pulling the pillow over his head. Considering how the music was bouncing off the walls, I didn't think that was going to help him. It didn't. In a few more seconds, he groaned and sat up again.

" There's no chance of sleeping with that going on," he grumped. Looking at me to be sure I was also wide awake, he said, "What would you think about getting up for breakfast?" I agreed we might just as well; sleep was not a possibility. Even conversation would have to be conducted at a higher decibel-level than normal. While Bill shaved and I reached into the refrigerator for the orange juice, eggs, and bacon Mom K stocked in for us while we were gone, I realized my feet were moving in time to the sounds! It was definitely honky-tonk. *And* it was definitely hymns.

After breakfast, Bill opened our apartment door to see if our first Sunday paper had arrived. The door facing ours opened. The man who lived there stepped into the hall for his paper at the same time. As the sounds emanated from our open door, he smiled and said to Bill, "Boy! The Sunday concert is a lot louder in your place than ours! It wakes *us* up each week, but it must blow YOU right out of bed!" Bill asked him, "You mean this happens every week?" "Yup!" he replied. "Millie over there used to work in a bar, so that's the only way she knows how to play piano — loud and honky-tonk! We never met her but the shop owner downstairs told us she got religion late in life. But it didn't turn her into a churchgoer. Instead, she just pounds out hymns on that damn' piano of hers every Sunday from 8:00 'til noon. You might as well get used to it!" Bill shook his head and came in to tell me the bad news.

Promptly at 8:00 a.m. each Sabbath, until we moved from that apartment, we heard Millie start thumping out praise on her old, upright piano. Probably always paid by the hour, Milled appeared to have a close relationship with the clock, to the very second! The weekly sounds went on (at a volume which should have made Millie's old fingers ache) 'til she stopped — often in mid-hymn! — *precisely* on the exact stroke of noon, when she judged she had paid sufficient dues to God. She rendered her selections with the same verve and volume with which she delivered dance music during her working years. Each weekend, even as we groaned when the sound awakened us, we had to smile as the style of Millie's playing painted visions in our heads of a beer mug bouncing merrily atop the rocking old piano as she enthusiastically praised the Lord with her fingers!

Millie was a neighborhood legend, but we only met her once in the 19 months we lived there. She had only retired in the past year. As we passed her door one morning just before our first Christmas, she emerged, a cigarette dangling from the corner of her crimsoned lips. She called hoarsely, "Hey there, you two! I'm your neighbor!" Lace-gloved hand outstretched, Millie tottered determinedly toward us on the icy sidewalk in dangerously high heels. I guessed she was close to 75, maybe lots more. Snow-white roots slashed her darkly-dyed hair, the bejeweled frames of her glasses sparkled in the cold sunshine, her heavy mascara, black penciled brows, bright rouge and dark crimson lipstick would have been perfect for a burlesque queen's evening stage performance. Millie's fashionable outfit had clearly been designed for a 20-year-old, while her mink wrap had seen better days about 50 years earlier. In a voice raspy from years of shouting over her own music in smoky bars, she roared accusingly, "You're new here, Girlie! — but welcome to the neighborhood! I know YOU, Young Fella, you grew up on this block! But you went and married a girl from another neighborhood — that could getcha hung for treason, ya know! — Jus' kiddin'!" she added, laughing a short bark in her gravelly voice. "Merry Christmas, Kiddies! Mind your p's and q's now!" at which she turned and risked a broken ankle tottering away on the icy walk on her astonishingly high heels. Meeting Millie was an experience akin to being run over by a bus.

HOME, SWEET HOME

Early that first Sunday evening "at home," there was a knock on our door. Having heard my father say at our wedding that the traditional Celtic way to bless a marriage is for the first visitors to arrive with food and drink, Bob and Alice were determined to be our initial callers. They brought us a new box of tea bags and a plate of homemade cookies, unaware that by "drink," Dad referred to an alcoholic beverage. But the magic of their good intentions worked for us regardless.

"I thought we'd blundered into a cave —" Alice said as I opened our door. "That downstairs hall is as dark as night!" She was right. The only so-called illumination was a bare 25-watt bulb hanging high above the door. "And then that stairway," added Bob, "you practically have to *feel* your way up to the landing!" He was correct, too. Climbing to the landing took one from dim to dark day or night. "At least we could see a pale bulb at the top when we headed up from there," Alice said. " — but why are those cans of turpentine on that bench next to your neighbor's door — and all those brushes hanging from it on hooks?" Bill told her, "The guy next door is a house painter. He soaks his brushes out there each night after work. Then when they're clean, he hangs them on those cup hooks to dry." He shrugged. " — What can we say? The guy has to work, and he has no place else to leave them."

We were eager to show off to our friends the nest we had so carefully feathered before our wedding. Our tiny living room seemed pretty crowded when they stepped inside. Even though its scant furnishings consisted of only the couch, floor lamp and console radio, two chairs and a lamp table, there was barely enough room between for opposing feet. We couldn't have squeezed more furniture into that room with a wedge and mallet!

Beyond the narrow living room was the apartment's skimpy single closet, with a chest of drawers and a clothes rod in its narrow depths. Past that, the very small second bedroom contained still-boxed wedding gifts, not yet unpacked for lack of space. Once homes were found for them, Bill planned to use that room for a study.

"C'mon, I'll give you the palace tour," Bill said. He led our friends into the dining-kitchen space. "Whoa! This floor slopes downhill! It makes me dizzy!" Bob was right — the floor *did* have a visible pitch. (We suspected an out-of-work deck builder might have installed it, since water ran down it just as on a deck. If I started washing at the top, I had to mop quickly to beat the water to the bottom end!) That floor always caused a moment of vertigo when guests encountered it for the first time.

The dinette/kitchen was only a little longer than our crowded living room. It held our "almost-new" table and four chairs, a tiny china cabinet, a small gas-fired space heater, as well as the refrigerator, range, and a wheeled worktable beside the stove. (Representing ingrained Depression-era thrift, that worktable was the diaper-changing table my father built when I was born!) A narrow bank of open shelves housed our everyday dishes, pots and pans. The sink, drain-board, and the water heater and tank filled the remaining wall space.

"Wow! This thing's taller than I am, "marveled Bob, looking up at the gargantuan tank. It had to be lighted with a match a good half-hour before even a scant supply of warm water became available for washing dishes. As for baths, experience soon taught us it took well over an hour to warm enough water to fill the tub just once. We learned to take shallow baths in the interest of reasonable bedtimes and impatience for new-married love!

"Let me show you the luxurious bathroom," Bill said, opening one of the two doors at the end of the room. It opened out since the commode (obviously an afterthought following the advent of indoor plumbing) occupied the space needed for it to swing the other way. Between the doorway and the window, the commode's width and the old-fashioned claw-foot tub's length fit to the eighth-inch! The tub's scratched, once-elegant, high-standing faucets guaranteed commode-sitters frequent electric zings when funny bones encountered them! Two lengthy metal towel bars opposite the tub lay in wait to bruise hips anytime, and in winter to flash-freeze wet flesh almost instantly. We had to sidle gingerly past them to towel dry in the small foot-space in front of the commode.

"There's no basin here," noticed Bob. "Where do you wash and shave?" "We wash hands under the bathtub faucets, " Bill said, touching them, "but we brush our teeth and I shave at the kitchen sink before Bea starts breakfast."

"And here's the master bedroom!" said Bill, carefully opening the door just 45 degrees to avoid bumping the corner of my dresser. Our double bed fit *exactly* between the end wall of the kitchen and the windowsill, with the doorframe nudging the near side of the headboard. With no space for a night table, Bill installed a shelf on the wall above the bed for our alarm clock. His tall chest stood beside the foot of the bed. Touching it, corner to corner, my dresser occupied the only remaining wall. Both bureaus' open drawers competed for the same space, so we could only access their contents by turns.

"You think this is too small?" kidded Bob, pushing past Bill to the little rectangle of floor space. " — Why, it's big enough for dancing!"

he declared, executing a couple of tap-dance steps in place.

I made tea, took the teapot, plates and cups into the living room, along with Alice's cookies. Bob asked Bill how he ever managed to find an apartment. "I lived just three doors down the street," Bill answered, "so when Mom heard from one of the shop owners that the tenants were moving out of town, I rushed right over to knock on their door. Other people had already asked about it, but I took the prize by offering to buy the entire apartment's contents so they wouldn't have to move it!

"I really thought it was all money down the drain," Bill went on, " — so much had to go down to the curb for the trash pick-up!" "*Including*," I elaborated, "an ancient ICEbox containing two bowls of elderly stewed tomatoes with furry green hats!" "Ye-e-ew, crummy!" Alice exclaimed, making a face.

"But it didn't turn out too badly, after all," Bill continued. "This living room set looked awful, but once Bea washed and polished these nice wide wood arms, we could see the finish is still really good!" "And my Aunt Evelyn taught me to make the new slip-covers," I added. "YOU made the slip-covers?" Alice was impressed. "Yes, with a lot of help," I told her, "but I think I'll be able to do them myself whenever I need to re-cover them."

"And look at this!" Bill pulled one of his college texts and a pad from under the chair. "I can even do my homework on the arm of this chair. It makes a pretty good desk." Tapping the edge of her saucer, Alice added, " — and these broad wood arms make handy snack tables, too."

"Then," Bill said, "there was an ugly old bureau in the back of the closet. It held the previous tenant's grungy sheets and towels. Mom washed, bleached, and cut them up, and we used them for scrub-cloths to clean this place. Everything was so dirty!" "I can imagine," Alice injected, "considering the moldy stewed tomatoes!" "But once Bea cleaned it out and re-lined the drawers," Bill told her, "all our new linens fit into it." I added, "With no linen closet here, that's really convenient." We all agreed that the amount Bill paid the former tenants was low enough to make the "keepers" a reasonable exchange.

Over time, that picture improved manyfold. After years of hard wear by our children and their friends in our family room, that living room furniture is so sturdy that it is *still* in use all these years later at our vacation place. With its newest slipcovers, it still looks great. As for the ugly old chest, daylight on it in a future move revealed a beautiful but badly battered old Eastlake bride's chest, which — after refinishing — claimed prominent pride of place in every home we occupied from then on.

"This building is as old as dirt," Bill told our friends, "so we expected some problems. But our bedroom *sure does* get pretty hot at night! The only ventilation is through three holes bored in the bottom of the storm window frame. I can't take it off the window because the hardware was painted in place so many years ago that it's rusted solidly in place under the paint. Even with the dinette windows open last night and a small fan on the corner of Bea's dresser, we baked in there!"

We approached that first night in our new home with anticipation until we discovered just how hot that bedroom was! We had to throw a blanket on the dinette floor near its opened double windows to bear the added heat of passion when we availed ourselves of our second opportunity to make love in our own home. The mattress on that second bedroom floor was much more comfortable!

But when winter came, we had the reverse problem. The little space heater made only the living room entirely comfortable. The closet was so cold that our chilly clothes rudely shocked us awake each morning. A test glass of water placed on the floor froze in the little bedroom, ending Bill's plans for a study; storage was the room's only practical use. The dinette and kitchen (closest to the heat source) were always too hot, especially when I was cooking, but in cold weather the apartment cooled drastically after dark. At least some of that kitchen heat seeped into the chilly bedroom and bathroom to make it bearable to undress, bathe, and slide into bed, but we found it necessary to make winter love under covers tented over us. With the heat of lovemaking, the bed finally warmed enough for us to sleep when we cuddled together spoon-fashion. However, morning trips to the bathroom took Spartan courage!

With new cabinets my father built around the sink and drain board, the tiny refinished china cabinet, newly-papered walls, scrubbed and freshly-painted woodwork, still-useful ruffled sheer curtains my mother rooted out of a trunk in her basement and Bill's mother's help to hang them, our apartment was readied for residency! Mom K offered to stock our refrigerator the day before our scheduled return from our honeymoon.

Despite its shortcomings, then known or soon made evident, we were very proud of our home. It was a place of our own, made beautiful by our own efforts and help from our families. "You were really lucky to find a place to move right into," Alice told us. "After four months at Bob's parents' place, we were sure glad to find a flat of our own!"

WILLARD, WILLARD! RUN QUICK!

On Monday, Bill and I returned to work and school. Tuesday, arriving home simultaneously from different bus stops, we started up the stairs arm in arm. But just then, the outside door was blasted open, slammed loudly against the wall. A red-faced neighbor boy panted, "Willard, Willard! Run! Quick!! The fire truck's at your folks'. Ma said I should tell ya your pa prob'ly had another stroke!" Bill turned and dashed past the boy with me right behind him.

Four firemen clustered about Dad's bed, trying their best to revive him. Mom stood motionless in the corner of the room, her hands over her mouth. Only moments after we dashed into the room, one of the firemen looked up and said, "No good, we'll have to pronounce 'im." Bill caught his mother as she sagged against the wall. I implored the men, "No! Don't stop!" The fireman who spoke looked at me sadly. "Honey, we can't do anything for 'im. 'E's gone." They pulled up the sheet and blanket, placed Dad's hands together on the top, smoothed the covers, then packed up their gear.

I saw the rescue team to the door and thanked them for their efforts. The one who made the dreaded pronouncement put his hand on my arm. "Tell your mother the medical examiner will be here real soon. We'll call 'im as soon as we get back to the station house."

Bill guided Mom to the living room, sat silently on the couch with his arms around her for several minutes, then knelt on the floor in front of her, taking her hands in his. "Mom," he said softly, "I have to call an undertaker. Who should I call?" Mom shrugged, too stunned to think. Bill thought a moment, then said, "My friend Barry from high school is in the funeral business with his dad now. Should I call him? I don't know anybody else." Mom nodded, pulled her hands out of Bill's, clasped them together so tightly her knuckles whitened.

Bill came back to tell her, "Mom, Barry will take care of everything. And I called your friend, Mamie. She'll be here in a second." Mamie arrived with her apron still tied around her waist, kneeled in front of Mom and took her hands. "Mamie, Mamie, he's gone, he's gone," Mom whispered hoarsely. She began to cry great, wracking sobs. Bill started forward, but Mamie had already enveloped Mom in her arms. They rocked back and forth together, both in tears.

Steve, Mamie's husband and Dad's daily partner at cards, arrived just then. He froze just inside the door, his eyes on Mom and Mamie. Then he squared his shoulders, turned to Bill and asked, "May I pay my last respects?" Bill led him to the bedroom. They were there for what seemed a long time.

The doorbell rang. It was the medical examiner. I led him back to the bedroom, where Bill ushered him solemnly in the door. Steve knelt beside his wife, holding both her and Mom tightly. Mom looked up, sighed the deepest sigh I had ever heard and said, "Well, we have to make the best of it, don't we? He hated being disabled and having all that trouble walking and talking." Looking up at me as if she had just noticed me there, she said, "And right after you came back from your honeymoon! This is so sad for you." That was just like Bill's mom, thinking immediately of others.

After the medical examiner left, Bill called Barry again. As the hearse pulled up, neighbors — who must have been keeping watch through parlor windows since the fire department's departure — rushed to the house. In those days, deaths usually occurred at home and neighbors immediately hurried to help. With no need for consultation, they quickly formed a closed circle around Mom as Dad's body was wheeled out the front door. After murmuring to Mom, some stayed to greet newcomers. Others hurried home to return quickly with platters of food, which had probably been intended for their families' suppers. More neighbors arrived. Some turned to the table as soon as they had spoken to Mom, others stood around unsure what to do next. But most stayed on for whatever comfort they could provide.

"We'll have to make some calls," Bill told me. "I can do that," I offered. Later, Bill said he thought he should stay at his mother's that night and I agreed. He walked me home to our apartment, wordlessly holding me very tightly and kissing me hard just outside the door. He started to turn away but then stopped to ask if I'd be all right. I assured him I would be, then went upstairs, unlocked our door and walked into our new home for the first night of my life I had ever spent alone.

As I entered, the telephone rang. It was Mother. "Is Bill with you?" she asked. "No, he thought he should stay there tonight." "Should Dad and I come in?" "No, there's no place here for you to sleep; I'll be alright," I told her. "Just come in tomorrow afternoon. Bill said the visitation won't start till about noon." We said goodnight and I crawled gratefully into bed. For some reason, I couldn't cry, even in sympathy for Mom and Bill. I wondered why, but then I fell asleep.

Mamie sat on a dining room chair all that night watching over Mom while she tossed fitfully in the bed she and Dad so recently shared. Steve dozed in a living room chair and Bill slept on the couch.

When I awakened in the morning, it all came back to me. "Poor Bill!" I exclaimed aloud, then "Poor *Mom!*"

On Thursday and Friday nights, different card-playing friends of Dad's sat on folding chairs, trying to stay awake facing the casket, while other friends of Mom's stayed with her in the bedroom, so Bill came home to sleep. He wrapped me tightly in his arms and fell asleep almost instantly.

I lay awake a long time both nights. I hadn't come to know Dad Keeber well. His speech problems interfered with communication. I recalled him sniffling aloud as I walked down the aisle with my father on our wedding day, his post-stroke emotions out of his control. I was often uneasy with him, unsure how to cope with that lack of control and my inability to understand most of his labored words.

Neighbors spoke so highly of a good man "who'd give you the shirt off his back," always full of fun. Friends spoke of weekly card parties where the ante was entrusted to Dad K, their "treasurer," to save for yearly group camping vacations. He was their Pied Piper for fishing expeditions and merriment. I felt sad about his death for Bill and Mom, but I had not known the man others were mourning.

Dad, a lapsed but still nominal Catholic, asked Mom to call a priest that last afternoon when he didn't feel well. He wanted forgiveness "just in case." The priest heard Dad's confession, gave him Last Rites, and departed. Not long after that, Dad breathed once deeply, then stopped altogether. Mom rushed to call the fire department, then hurried back to the bedroom to lean over the bed, hugging Dad, calling his name over and over, trying to wake him until the fire department arrived. It was the rescue team's truck that alerted the next-door neighbor to send her boy running for Bill.

That next morning, when I walked down the street to the house, I noticed a black wreath on the front door. It must have been placed there the previous evening when the hearse came for Dad's body. Bill and Mom were at Barry's to make arrangements. While they were gone, the funeral director's men arrived to prepare the house. They carried all the living room furniture to the basement, leaving one comfortable armchair for Mom. They set a lengthy rough wooden stand against the wall where the couch had been, covered it with black cloth and placed folding chairs around the room. When Bill and Mom returned, Bill led his mother to the bedroom so she wouldn't need to watch the activity.

The hearse arrived and the men placed the casket on the long fabric-covered support. Barry positioned vases of flowers at each end, then opened it to reveal Dad clothed in his good suit, shirt and tie he wore at our wedding. A spray of red roses was placed between his hands, bearing two ribbons, lettered "Dearest Husband" and "Dear Dad." Finally, the men placed a kneeler in front of the casket. Mamie went to the bedroom to tell Mom and Bill to come out.

Widow and son approached the casket, Bill's hand firmly at Mom's elbow, Mamie on her other side. Mom shivered, clenched her jaw and fists, but stood erect. As she looked at her husband of many years, I saw a single tear travel down her pale cheek. Bill stood staunchly dry-eyed, almost at military attention. A few neighbors, having seen the hearse arrive, quietly opened the door and entered. After Bill led his mother to her chair, a stream of neighbors said their goodbyes to Dad and spoke softly to Mom and Bill.

A steady parade of people called by me or notified by the obituary in the Buffalo Evening News filled the house that afternoon and evening and for the next two days. Neighbors Bill's mother knew only by sight and wave stopped in upon seeing the black wreath, some of them carrying casseroles. Mom sat there all day every day, except when Bill ushered her to the kitchen for Mamie to encourage her to eat a few bites. But she quickly returned to the living room as if drawn by a magnet. Bill kept turning to the coffin, staring at his father intently, silently.

I wondered what Bill was burying beneath his solicitous attention to Mom, his serious demeanor, his pale complexion ever since that fateful, "Willard, Willard, Run! Quick!" How could he bear to look on his father's body so soon after steeling himself to take clothes and rations and ammunition for his own survival from the bodies of men frozen in the Ardennes' snow? Were his worries that his "missing in action" report contributed to his father's first stroke weighing on him now? What was he feeling inside? I ached to comfort him, but he didn't know how to let me in to his emotions.

THE FUNERAL

At 10:00 a.m. that Saturday morning, Barry arrived with the stranger-priest who had given Dad Last Rites. Mom's chair and all the folding chairs had already been moved to the basement. Mom was pale but composed with Bill at her side in front of the casket, stiffly erect. I stood on her other side, Mamie and Steve behind us. In the living room were crowded friends, neighbors, my parents, aunts, uncles. People were jammed tightly together there, in the dining room, front entry hall, and as many as three to a step on the hall staircase overlooking the living room. Latecomers stood outside on the porch and front steps.

The priest conducted the service but I couldn't understand the Latin, nor could Mom or Bill, all three of us standing silent, motionless. Finally, the priest faced the casket, made the sign of the cross, then wordlessly, head bowed, he left the house, people parting for him to pass. Mom and I were ushered into the funeral director's limousine. Bill helped to carry out the casket, then sat beside Mom. She was silent and dry-eyed, her jaw set, her gaze locked on the hearse.

At the cemetery, three folding chairs waited in a row facing the open grave, with a few more behind for those unable to stand. The priest, who arrived there ahead of us, commenced the short graveside service — in Latin, of course. Bill, Mom and I could hear a few people behind us mumbling in response to the priest's words. After concluding his last prayer, he stood to one side with his head bowed. Barry gave Mom a handful of dirt, then led her to the edge of the grave. Bill kept his arm firmly around her shoulder.

Mom winced, shuddered, closed her eyes and tightened her fists reflexively while the metal cranks shrieked and groaned, lowering the casket on ropes into the abyss. She looked down to filter the soil through her fingers onto the casket far below, then closed them tightly again. The priest said another prayer, a few quiet, perfunctory words to Mom and Bill, ignored me as if I weren't there, then turned and left. I hated him so fiercely for his coldness to Mom, it's a wonder he didn't wince as he passed me! It wasn't until many years later that it occurred to me he might have been as uncomfortable as we were. He was young and probably had no idea what to say to non-Catholic relatives.

As the limousine turned toward the gate, Mom twisted around to look back. "It's a pretty spot, isn't it, looking over that little lake?" she said. "Will always loved the water and fishing. I hope he likes it here." Bill registered a moment of surprise, then told her, "I'm sure he will, Mom." Mom looked away from the gravesite, keeping her eyes front and center for the trip back home.

The funeral director's men descended the instant we left for the cemetery. In the short time we were gone, they returned all the furniture to the living room. The house looked just as it did before Dad died except for the flowers on every table and on top of the china cabinet — and that black wreath on the front door to tell passers-by to walk respectfully past that home Death had visited. Barry told Mom to dispose of it after the traditional week's time. When we returned, friends were already there with bowls of potato salad, platters of cold meat and cheese, breads, butter, mayonnaise and mustard to share. Funeral luncheons then were do-it-yourself events for those who attended.

Mom bustled about making sure everyone had a full plate,

heaping on seconds if they'd have them. She kept moving so nobody had a chance to say much to her. Finally, when empty plates crowded the dining room table, Mom, standing, stopped for a steaming cup of coffee. She quickly drank down the hot brew, took a deep breath, then turned to the people gathered there and said firmly, "Thank you for everything you've done for Will and me. But now it's time for you all to get back to your own lives." She added determinedly, "I'm going to be alright."

She looked around once more and said, "I appreciate all you've done, but now I have to start learning how to get along without Will." She picked up plates. Mamie and I did, too. Mom carried them to the kitchen sink to put them down, followed closely by Mamie, Bill and me. Mom turned and clasped Bill and me close, then said, almost sternly, "You two go on home! You're newly married; you need time together. I'm so grateful Will was able to see you married, Bea. Now — I have roomers upstairs to look after, laundry to do and beds to make up; I've neglected them too long." With that, she pushed us away, "Go! Go back to your own home!" Mamie left the kitchen to usher out others who remained in the dining and living rooms.

Mom took Bill's and my arms and walked us to the front door. She said again, "Now go on home. I'll be fine." We hesitated. Mamie stood beside her, wringing her hands. Mom said to her, "Mamie, you've been so good to me. But it's time for you and Steve to get back to your own lives."

Steve put his hand on Mamie's shoulder, pushing her gently toward the door. He reached for Bill's hand to say formally, "My condolences on your loss of your father, Willard." Without a word, he grasped Mom's shoulders and squeezed them, turned to open the door, held it while Bill and I quietly went through, then he and Mamie followed us out. Mom watched us all walk down the front steps, then she closed the door with a quiet click. Bill told Mamie and Steve, "I'll come back in a little while to be sure she's alright." They walked slowly down the block toward their own home, while Bill and I turned toward ours.

When we reached our apartment, Bill yawned. "You know, I'm really tired," he said. "Try to nap then," I told him. "Only if you'll come with me," he replied. We walked into the bedroom hand in hand, undressed, and slid naked between the sheets. I faced Bill, stroking his face for a moment, unsure what to say to him. He kissed me lightly, then more insistently. Wordlessly, we made love.

Afterwards, Bill turned me over and pulled me close against him so we could cuddle. His breath sounded rough in my ears. Then his breathing became even and smooth as he slept. With his arms wrapped tightly around me, I fell asleep, too, only waking when Bill threw back the covers, telling me, "I'd better go check on Mom." Sitting on the bed, I watched him dress. He leaned over, kissed me gently, said, "Don't go away, now!"

Bill returned with a large paper bag and a puzzled expression. "The dining room and kitchen were all cleaned up and Mom was in the basement hanging wash," he said wonderingly. "When I found her there, she said, 'Willard, I'm glad you came back. There's far too much food in the refrigerator. Come upstairs with me. I want you to take some of it home.' She opened the door and began putting containers on the table. I told her, 'Mom, there are only two of us!' 'Well, *somebody* has to eat up all this food before it spoils!' she told me, and went right on putting stuff into the bag. Then she said, 'Here, go on home now and have a good hot meal. It will only take Bea a few minutes to warm some of that in the oven.' She almost pushed me out the door! I'll bet by now she's back in the basement hanging wash!" He looked puzzled.

"Your mother has been so strong all through your father's failing health and the funeral," I told him. "Maybe she needs quiet time by herself to do 'normal' things like laundry. I'll start to warm up some of this. We need to eat something, then get to bed early. I have to do laundry tomorrow before work on Monday, and you should probably read ahead before classes on Monday. You've missed two weeks now instead of just the one you expected to miss for our honeymoon." "Do you think I should leave Mom alone all night?" Bill asked. "I don't think you have a choice," I said. "She made it clear she wanted everyone out of the house except the roomers. I'll call when some of this food is hot to tell her we need her to help eat it. It IS too much for us. Maybe she will."

She did, arriving in her housedress with her apron still on, as if she could barely spare the time. Finishing quickly, she rose from our table to start washing up. To my, "Oh, don't, Mom! I'll do that!" she waved me away. "I like being busy. You probably need to lay out whatever you'll wear to work tomorrow." "Mom, tomorrow's Sunday," I replied. "I don't go to work till Monday. In fact, I need to come to your house tomorrow to do laundry." "Oh!" she said. "I lost track of the days, didn't I? Well then, dry these dishes while I finish washing, then I'm going home. Tomorrow, bring over your laundry and we'll do it together."

LAUNDRY LESSONS

The next morning, I walked down the street to Mom's with our laundry in a large bag. The black wreath no longer hung at the front door. It was on a chair in the kitchen.

Attaching a hose to the laundry tub faucet, Mom showed me how to fill her washing machine, where to plug it in to start the motor, how much to put into the machine. After the clothes had agitated for the required time, she fed the first of the wet clothes through the wringer into the two concrete rinse tubs she filled with warm and cool water, then lastly, into a basket — then let me follow suit with the rest of them. She demonstrated how to boil starch for shirt collars and cuffs and how to use it, then watched me do that task. Next, she thinned the starch for the shirt bodies, showed me how to dip one in it and watched over me as I finished that job. Finally, she handed me the basket of all the clean clothes and instructed me to hang everything on the lines in the back yard while she took down her own dried laundry from the basement lines. " — then come back in," she said.

When I returned, Mom said, "Now I'll show you how I dampen things for ironing." She demonstrated on her own laundry, then said, "You and Willard come to dinner tomorrow after work and school. Then

Willard can study while we get started on your ironing." I had confessed to her before the wedding that Mother never taught me to do laundry at home. "I think your wash will be dry outside in about two hours today with the breeze. Bring it back inside then so you can dampen it." With that, she gently ushered me up the stairs.

Two hours later, I learned the correct way to hang wash. After I left, Mom went outside, un-pegged starched collars to re-hang shirts by their tails. She took down the individual socks I hung higgledy-piggledy from their tops here and there on the line, paired them, then re-hung them, toes together, one peg per pair so I could efficiently put together each dry pair as I took them off the line. Instead of flung over the line every which way, Bill's shorts and my undies hung neatly side by side, each sharing a peg with the next one, dancing in the breeze like the Rockettes' chorus line we'd seen on our honeymoon.

I took down the dried wash, making a mental note of how each item was hung on the line, and folded everything into the basket Mom left beneath the clothesline. At the side door, I knocked and went in. Mom was coming down the back stairs to the kitchen. "I just changed all the roomers' beds," she told me. "Let's go dampen whatever needs to be ironed." I followed her to the basement again. "Here!" She handed me the bottle with a shaker top. "Try doing it the way I showed you." Awkwardly, I shook moisture onto a pillowcase, embarrassed when I saw I was leaving some places too damp, others too dry. Mom assured me it would even itself out. I finished the rest and she packed it all into an oilcloth-lined basket, covering it with another oilcloth.

"Now come back for dinner after work tomorrow and we'll start the ironing," she told me. Before I left, I turned to hug her and thank her for showing me how to do things. She hugged me back warmly.

We did go to Mom's for dinner the next day. All the vases of flowers were gone and so was the black wreath. Bill helped us clear the table to spread out his books and start on his homework. Mom and I went to the basement so she could teach me the rudiments of ironing. Slowly, I began pushing the iron back and forth. Mom praised my careful efforts, reaching out to pull and tug at fabric to even it out ahead of my iron – teaching me how. As time went on, I did learn to wash and iron well, thanks to Mom's tutoring. And she never for a moment gave me reason to feel foolish about what I didn't know.

CULINARY ARTS 101

"What's that smell? It's enough to gag a maggot!" Bill exclaimed as he ran in the door, alarmed. I had already turned on a fan and was frantically opening windows, but it didn't help much.

Mother was so skilled in an office, but it was fortunate she refrained from teaching me her cooking techniques even though I was not yet a cook when I married. Instead, my patient, tactful mother-in-law, just three doors down the street from us became my on-call cookbook. With her help, I learned to prepare the sort of German-style fare my husband loved. But — I had a number of misadventures during my introduction to the culinary arts.

The first place I went awry was in trying to make lunches for us to carry to school and work after I used up all the leftover sliced meat and cheese from the funeral. It didn't occur to me I might need supervision when I planned to make egg salad for sandwiches, but it would have helped! As soon as I walked into the apartment, I put eggs on the stove to come to a boil, then went into the bedroom to change from my office outfit into a housedress. Noticing a new homemaking magazine left on my bedroom dresser the previous evening, I sat on the edge of the bed reading the delicious-sounding recipes.

As the pot boiled dry, eggshells burst. Their scorched contents spattered all over the range and the wall behind it. Finally alerted by the popping sounds, I raced into the kitchen just before Bill came home. He was right. The smell was really awful — so bad it made our eyes water!

We opened windows, propped open our apartment door and the one downstairs. Bill ran to borrow extra fans from his mother. Mom K suggested we share her freshly made meat loaf that night. We were grateful to escape the stench. By bedtime, the odor had dissipated enough for us to sleep in the apartment without gagging. But it took the better part of a week, opening windows and running fans each evening, to disperse all remaining olfactory reminders of the episode.

Then there was the alarm clock mystery. As a new cooking student, everything took me a long time to accomplish. Sometimes, after work, I could not manage to produce a complete dinner 'til late in the evening. Bill, whose stomach grumbled exactly on the dot at breakfast, lunch and dinner times, was remarkably patient with my efforts, giving me plenty of room to learn, complimenting me on whatever I managed to put on the table. But he insisted on taking over the bedtime winding of our alarm clock after the morning we awakened at 9:00 a.m., making us late for class and work.

Exhausted after my painstakingly slow, unskilled labors at the stove and sink the previous evening, I fell into bed as soon as I completed those chores. Bill stayed up to study. I was positive I had wound our Big Ben alarm clock, but it still didn't awaken us on time. We learned why when we noticed the quart of milk on the shelf above our bed; the clock was chilling in the refrigerator.

I also needed tutelage in how to shop for groceries. Uncle Bill's meat and grocery store was where Mum obtained her needs. I had never even seen the inside of one of those new-fangled supermarkets before our wedding. They made my uncle so angry the way they undercut his prices that I almost felt guilty shopping there. But his store was across town from our apartment. Without a car, I had to patronize local ones.

Fortunately, Bill knew his way around both the kitchen and market from helping his mother. Prudently, he offered to shop with me on weekends.

On one of our early trips to the meat counter, Bill picked up what looked like a very fat sausage. "What's that?" I asked. "Smoked beef tongue," he answered. "It's very good, sort of like ham." I had never even heard of beef tongue. I asked him, "How's it prepared?"

"Oh, it's easy," he responded. "You just simmer it in water till it's tender, then you serve thin slices with mustard on the side. You can cook potatoes and vegetables in the same pot. When you get down to the small bones at the base of the tongue, you cut away the bones, and grind up the scraps of meat. If you add pickle relish and mayo, it makes great sandwich spread. You can use the cooking water to make split pea or lentil soup, too." That sounded both economical enough for our budget and simple enough for my rudimentary skills, so I told Bill to place it in our basket.

At home, I unwrapped the meat. First off was a cellophane cover, revealing a tight mesh wrap. I cut that away, then placed the fat sausage in a pot of cold water. Covering the pot, I turned the flame on high and went to the living room, where Bill was studying, to read with him while I awaited sounds of the lid's dancing.

When I heard the cheerful rattle, I returned to the kitchen, picked up a potholder to lift the cover, then … the pot lid went clattering across the room! That and my shriek rudely interrupted Bill's studies. Dashing into the kitchen, he found me in front of the stove, covering my face with both hands. The meat, freed of its tight wraps, swelled and opened up in the hot water. It no longer resembled a fat sausage. It was now a submerged monster sticking out its tongue at me!

I ran into the living room, refusing to return to the kitchen "with that ugly thing in there!" Without a word, Bill turned off the burner, found the flung potholder and lid, and carried the cook-pot down the street to his mother. Returning, he noted casually, carefully without a trace of a smile, that we'd have dinner at his mother's that evening.

The next time I saw the tongue, neat pink slices circled a small pressed-glass bowl of mustard, all atop a bed of fresh dark green Romaine lettuce leaves on one of my mother-in-law's pretty platters. Accompanying the platter were bowls of boiled potatoes, carrots and a salad of crisp mixed greens.

I helped myself to salad, potatoes and carrots, then, hungry, I watched Bill and his mother transferring meat to their plates, adding dollops of mustard to each slice. Tentatively, I took one, spread mustard thinly over it, cut off a bite-sized piece and tasted. It was delicious! I reached for another slice, then more. Once I knew how good smoked tongue tasted, I overcame my resistance to cooking it. Bill and I enjoyed it often, and loved the sandwich spread that became its final end. In between, we had lentil or split pea soup for weekend lunches.

The August after our June wedding, I suggested that Mom come to our apartment for her birthday dinner. I knew I was not yet up to a "company dinner," but I didn't want Mom to spend her first birthday as a widow alone. Mom protested that it would be too tiring for me to make a party dinner after work so she asked us to her house instead. Relieved, I insisted I could at least provide the cake. After all, how difficult could a boxed cake mix be?

I made that the evening before and only had to frost it after work and before the birthday dinner. It wasn't the chocolate cake mix that was the problem. It was the seven-minute-icing I tried to make, following the directions in my new *Joy of Cooking* cookbook. According to *Joy*, this would be a "very fluffy, delightful icing that never fails." She was wrong! Whatever I did or did not do, the concoction never attained a fluffy consistency. Well past the seven minutes prescribed in the recipe, it became more and more sticky and gooey. The beater groaned as it struggled through the white glue.

When I called the painter's wife from across the hall, she examined the sluggish mess, said it didn't look like any icing she ever made. She suggested I stop beating and try to spread it on the cake, then left me to my fate. As I did that, the cake broke apart into three pieces. Bill thought of pinning the pieces together with toothpicks. We did that, then he held the pieces firmly together while I spread icing on the top. It adhered, but pulled away some of the surface of the cake to form chocolate-crumb curls atop the frosting.

It was already past time for us to be at Bill's mom's. Not daring to attempt to frost the sides, we just carried my sorry-looking offering down the street on a plate. As we entered the kitchen door, Mom looked at the cake wide-eyed, but collected herself to say, "Oh, my birthday cake! THANK you! I'll put it over here for now. Dinner is already on the table. Come on!"

We trooped into the dining room to enjoy a meal of sauerbraten, sauerkraut, rot kraut, mashed potatoes, green beans, and fresh salad. I partook so enthusiastically I had to loosen my belt. After the meal, my mother-in-law excused herself to make coffee. When I rose to help, she told me not to bother — said she'd only be a few minutes.

In a short time, she brought in the coffee pot and cake plates. She returned to the kitchen and came back with a tray, on which sat three pretty glass bowls, large pieces of cake in each, swimming in warm butterscotch pudding. There was a candle on each brown island. I saw no trace of that seven-minute icing. Mom set a bowl on each cake plate. Bill lighted the candles and we sang "Happy Birthday." Mom closed her eyes, made a wish, then blew out the three candles. The cake and the pudding were both delicious. — I wondered if Mom wished her son had married a girl who could cook.

I did learn to cook. My husband enjoyed what I made. In fact, he enjoyed it so much that the beautiful bones I had so admired in his craggy face at first acquaintance became well concealed. But *I* knew they were there through all the years of our marriage!

GAIL ELIZABETH – AND A COUPLE OF OTHER ISSUES
PUSS-PUSS

One Friday bedtime, when October was beginning to chill the outside air, our bedroom was still uncomfortably warm from cooking. To provide enough ventilation to sleep, we propped open the apartment door to the length of the chain lock by inserting a couple of Bill's textbooks into the space. We didn't set the alarm clock since we planned to sleep late the next morning.

About dawn, I was disturbed by a recurring squeak. I tried to ignore it, but it continued to annoy. I rolled onto my back — and felt a sudden weight on my chest. My eyes opened wide in alarm as I looked into the face of a tiger! But when my morning vision cleared, I realized it was only a tiger-striped kitten. Reaching out to stroke the little creature, I felt its ribs. It must be hungry. I tried to arise without disturbing Bill, but the insistent noise had disturbed him, too.

"Where are you going?" he mumbled. "To heat some milk for this kitten," I answered. "Kitten! Where?" Bill opened his eyes. "Right here. She's a skinny little thing; she must be hungry." She purred and meowed intermittently while Bill petted her till I returned with a saucer of milk.

Awake by then, Bill and I decided to get up for breakfast. The kitten insistently wound herself around my ankles as I tried to cook. Then she jumped onto Bill's lap to attempt to climb onto the table. He moved his chair closer to block her way until he finished and placed his breakfast plate on the floor, with its last scraps of scrambled eggs. In seconds, it was empty and polished. My scraps, too, were quickly devoured. "She must not have a home, considering the way her ribs show. Do you want to keep her?" Bill asked. "I think we've already been adopted," I replied.

Cans of cat food were added to our shopping lists. We named her Puss-Puss. She happily became a lap cat, purring on Bill's lap while he wrote his homework, or on mine beneath a book I was reading. Puss-Puss monopolized our attention for the next 11 months.

GAIL ELIZABETH

Before we married, Bill and I made plans to have a large family — *after* he graduated from college and had a good start in his new career. But then-chancy birth control and new-married passion resulted in the birth of our daughter, Gail Elizabeth, on September 21st, 1949, only a year-and-a-quarter after our wedding. Despite the financial inconvenience, Bill and I were ecstatic at beginning the family we wanted.

"I'm a little nervous about being responsible for a baby," I confessed to Bill. "Being the youngest cousin in my whole family, I have no experience with babies." "Oh, you'll learn fast!" he assured me, "and Mom will help. But I've had you all to myself up till now. I wonder what it will be like having to share you with a baby?" Although apprehensive about the end of our "couple-hood," we were both excited about our impending parenthood.

I researched the subject of birthing with great interest. Having heard of "natural childbirth" from a friend, I found an obstetrician willing to work with patients through this new delivery style. I was my physician's second patient for the pioneering process. Bill came with me to "interview" the new doctor to be sure he was the right one to deliver our baby. He and Bill thought much alike and were very comfortable with each other. I found Dr. Lechner warm and pleasant. He was definitely the right one to usher our baby into the world.

We were given a book to read — *Natural Childbirth*, by Dr. Grantly Dick Reade. There were no classes then, no support groups, no exercise training, no coaching lessons for husbands. We simply read the book to learn about cooperative labor, controlled breathing, husband as coach and helper in accomplishing painless delivery. Dr. Lechner encouraged Bill to plan to stay with me during labor, even though all hospitals banned fathers from delivery rooms at that time. We were excited about doing this whole thing together. Bill told me, "You may be the one who's pregnant, but I'm glad there's a way for me to do *my* share in getting our baby here!"

I was encouraged to bring a list of questions each time I visited the doctor. My list usually contained at least as many questions of Bill's as mine. I once tested Dr. Lechner with an exceptionally lengthy list. Dr. L, who spoke with a slight Austrian accent, reached over, plucked from my hand the paper from which I was reading. "It iss simple," he said soothingly, "The answers are all the same — becoss you are haffing a baby!"

As the pregnancy wore on, Bill liked to put his hand or ear on my abdomen to feel the baby move. When we settled into bed, he'd say, mock-sternly, leaning in close to my belly, "OK there, Kiddo. It's bedtime. We have to get up early, so it's time for you to pack in the night life!"

Gail was due September first. Bill hovered, my mother, father and grandmother hovered, Mom Keeber hovered. But that date came and went. I was huge and became more so as days passed. About mid-month, Alice came to the house with a small box tied with pink and blue ribbons. "Oh, an early baby gift!" I exclaimed delightedly. "No, it's actually for you," said Alice. "Go ahead and open it." When I tore away the paper and opened the box, I found ... a can opener! Bill threw his head back and laughed so hard! "Can't you take a hint?" he prodded.

Neither that strong suggestion nor anything else encouraged labor to begin. More days passed. Bill, worried, called Dr. L, who told him casually that babies arrive when babies are good and ready to travel and no sooner.

On September 21st, I had come to suspect I would never have a baby — just an extended belly forever. I drank a cola the night before, and, unwilling to be disappointed, decided I must be suffering gaseous indigestion. I disturbed Bill when I arose to walk the floor, so he started timing what I was calling "gas cramps." Pooh-poohing his activity, I assured him that what I was feeling was nothing at *all* like labor as described in the book. Still, he kept making notations. Finally, he told me, "These contractions —" "Cramps!" I injected. "These *whatevers* are averaging three minutes apart. I'm calling the doctor!" Dr. L said "Yes, she's definitely in labor. The contractions seem very close! Take her to the hospital right away. I'll meet your there."

Bill called Bob, who had volunteered to drive us to the hospital since we had no car. A milkman, he was at the dairy at 6:30 a.m. loading his milk for delivery. Alice gave us the telephone number. Leaving his truck half-loaded, Bob rushed to our apartment in his car to run us to the hospital. Then he hurried back to the dairy to start his day's work.

Bill ushered me through the hospital door as if I were fragile crystal. When the intake nurse began taking down information, Bill insistently injected, "You know, the contractions were only three minutes apart before we left home! Do you think she should be sitting here answering all these questions?" The nurse looked at him in surprise and told me, "You need to be in a room right away! Your husband can finish giving me this information." "But Dr. Lechner promised that my husband could stay with me through labor!" I protested. "He did arrange for that," she said. "However, we need to prep you. Your husband may come see you in just a few minutes."

I was loaded onto a gurney and rushed down the hall by another nurse. After a quick examination, she said, "Oh my! We have to get you right into Delivery!" I protested that Bill was supposed to be with me during labor. "No time for that now!" exclaimed the nurse and started *running* my gurney down the hall at breakneck speed. Bill, approaching the labor room with his coat over his arm, stood back against the wall, wide-eyed as the nurse raced me past him. I looked at him in dismay, but he disappeared quickly from my sight.

I was barely deposited in Delivery when Gail made her appearance. Dr. L had a mirror placed so I could see her arrival. I so wished Bill could have been there with me! But he could not see the baby or me until I was wheeled into Recovery with Gail resting comfortably on my belly.

Her head felt velvety-smooth as I stroked what felt and looked like peach fuzz. Bill stroked her head, too, with a look of wonder and delight on his face. Bill was never a man to speak easily of his emotions, but I noticed tell-tale moisture in his eyes as he touched Gail.

"I was so worried when they ran you past me!" he said. "I thought something was wrong." He kept touching my shoulder, my cheek, then Gail's soft hair. A nurse bustled in and whisked her away. "Time for Babykins' bath!"

Bill leaned over the bed to kiss me. "Oh Bill!" I told him. "I wish you could have been there! She simply slipped out like magic. It wasn't very uncomfortable at all. The doctor told me to take a deep breath and push, and there she was. I watched it all in the mirror. Isn't she beautiful?" "Yes, she IS," Bill replied in a voice filled with awe, looking toward the door through which she disappeared. "I can't believe she's here already. You delivered her just as if you do this every day for a living!" Then he added, "I love you so much! I would never have forgiven myself if you had a problem!"

"Forgive *yourself!*" I burst out. "Bill Keeber! THIS was a cooperative endeavor and don't you forget it!" "I know," he said, "but I kept thinking that if I hadn't gotten you pregnant, you wouldn't be having a problem.'" "Well, I wasn't having a *'problem,'* I was having our BABY! Isn't she wonderful?"

"She sure is," he agreed. Then, with a very serious expression, he added, "and so are you." A nurse soon stuck her head in the door to say, "Come with me, Dad. You can see your little girl now." Bill turned to follow the nurse, telling me, "I'll be right back. Don't go away, now!"

When Bill returned, he told me, "She's the prettiest baby in the whole nursery!" "You couldn't be a little prejudiced in her favor, could you?" I teased. "Oh no!" Bill answered seriously. "She really *is!*" By that time, my eyelids were heavy and I dozed off and on. Bill said, "They told me I have to leave now, but I'll be back this afternoon at visiting hours."

Some months later, we were at a party also attended by an obstetrical nurse. She heard we were first-time parents so she asked solicitously how bad the delivery had been. "Oh, it wasn't anything," I responded. "I had her by natural childbirth." "Oh, that's that silly new idea that mothers can just breathe right and they'll have no pain," she exclaimed disdainfully. "What nonsense! I've been an obstetrical nurse for years and I guarantee no birth ever occurs without pain. You were just so thrilled with your baby that you forgot about it." Nothing I could say convinced her I truly had Gail with only what I termed "discomfort" from "indigestion." She seemed offended that I disagreed with her years of experience.

The first evening we had Gail at home, our bedroom's small rectangle of floor space nicely accommodated her wheeled basket until we needed to access our bed. Then we trundled the basket uphill into the dining area. When the baby disturbed in the night, I bumbled out of bed and immediately bumped into the basket, right in our bedroom doorway. Gail's wake-up movements propelled her down-deck all the way to our bedroom! We learned to block her wheels.

MUTINY IN THE RANKS!

The next morning, Bill's mother brought our cat home after caring for her while I was in the hospital. With assured dignity, Puss-puss strolled regally around the apartment as if to say, "All's well. The queen is now in residence." Used to our undivided attention, she objected loudly when she saw Gail in my arms. Completely ignoring Bill's lap, she was determined to wrest *all* of my attention from this noisy interloper. She repeatedly tried to claw her way past Gail to nuzzle my face. When I pushed her down, she paced back and forth at my feet, her tail twitching. As soon as I put Gail into her basket, Puss-Puss jumped into it, tail swishing, yowling her dislike of the baby. We removed her and scolded sternly. But the second I turned away, she jumped back into the basket, her hackles raised.

We had a serious territorial dispute on our hands! We had to keep Puss-Puss in the small bedroom whenever we could not actively pet or play with her. But every time we let her out, she headed straight for Gail's basket, her tail an upright battle flag! It quickly became clear that Puss-Puss was not prepared to live equably with our daughter. For Gail's safety, we needed to find our pet a good home.

It turned out that the mother of one of Bill's schoolmates had recently lost her cat and would be delighted with a new one. In a secure box, Bill took Puss-Puss to her new residence. Our friend's mother opened the box, lifted out our cat, cuddled her lovingly and offered her a "tasty treat." Puss-Puss settled into her lap contentedly, as if to say, "I can see I'll be appreciated *here*." Bill fondly patted her head before he left, but she paid him no attention at all; Puss-Puss would never miss us for a moment in her new home. Gail was safe from her jealousy.

BUT STILL NO PEACE?

The cat was gone, but that did not bring peace to the household. Gail suffered colic for her first few weeks. We suffered sleeplessness as she wailed her unhappiness. Despite trying everything Dr. Lechner, Bill's mother, my mother, my grandmother suggested, tears were the order of the day — and night.

Bill and I, thoroughly exhausted, were very grateful when, between two and three months of age, Gail outgrew that stage and began to sleep quietly for three or four hours between feedings. After a couple of weeks of reasonable sleep, we mostly forgot the trial of walking our baby up and down our kitchen/dining room night after sleepless night. We were finally able to just enjoy our baby girl.

"You know, I worried a little that I'd mind having to share you," Bill confessed. "But I love to see her in your arms. When you look at her, you just glow! It makes me feel so good."

WHAT NEXT?

But another problem was soon to arise — one we never envisioned. We really loved our cozy little apartment despite its shortcomings. It was our post-honeymoon nest where we made new-married love to the suggestive squeals of mice also making whoopee in the attic above our bed. It was where I learned to cook and keep house. It was the haven to which we brought our first-born, which boasted the strange floor where we walked her — literally — up and downhill night after night when her colic kept us all awake.

In early December, when Gail was just past two months old, the upholsterer in the shop downstairs tossed furniture stuffing into his capacious stove. The straw exploded angrily into flames. They quickly clawed their way up the flue between our wall and Millie's apartment. The snap-on cover masking an unused stovepipe access to the chimney blew out with force, flaming straw pouring out behind it!

No time to telephone for help — the emergency was upon us! Throwing a blanket over Gail's basket to shield her from the floating fires, I frantically pounded out mini-blazes on the kitchen floor, walls and stovetop with a broom and dishtowels. At last, hearing my shrieks and stamping from upstairs, the upholsterer realized what was happening behind the closed door of his stove. He threw buckets of water into it, belatedly dousing the fire. The supply of burning straw dwindled. The emergency ended, but the kitchen was smoky and littered with charred straw.

With the upholsterer's stove on the ground floor beneath us, and paintbrushes soaking in turpentine at our entry door, we realized our haven was, in reality, a firetrap. With our baby's safety to consider, we had no choice but to seek a new place to live.

HAPPY NEW YEAR, SWEETHEART (1950)

Bill quickly found our second home just half a block down the street. On his way home from school, he saw a "For Rent" sign being placed in a front window — what unbelievable luck and good timing! It was the vacant lower flat in a house owned by a 94-year-old gentleman and his spinster daughter, living together upstairs. The flat was far too large for us with two parlors and three bedrooms, but the rent was reasonable, so we immediately signed a one-year lease. We had no problem subletting our apartment.

We moved on December 31st. It snowed lightly on and off all that gray day. Early in the morning, with our two mothers and Gail at the new flat, my father took up his post in our apartment. Dad's job was to pack in newspapers all items small enough to fit into bushel baskets and cardboard boxes.

Bill and I carried them downstairs, loaded them two at a time onto Bill's boyhood express wagon. Bill pulled the wagon down the nearest driveway into the snow-slushy street. I walked beside it steadying the baskets or boxes so they wouldn't bounce off. Crossing the busy intersection at our corner, we trundled the wagon a half-block more to haul it up the nearest driveway to our flat's front steps. Turning over filled baskets to our mothers, we claimed empties they had unpacked to exchange with Dad for more full ones. I don't know how many trips we made with the wagon, but it felt like a never-ending treadmill.

After lunch, the movers we hired to transfer the refrigerator and range arrived at the apartment to maneuver them down that narrow stairway and install them in the new location. The rest of the furniture was our job.

Bill and I removed the cushions from the living room set, carried the frames, one by one, down the stairs to balance on two-by-fours laid lengthways on the wagon for the trip down the street. Bill had to tie a rope to the wagon's handle to move all the large items of furniture since they seriously overlapped the wagon's dimensions. At our destination, we carried each piece up the front steps and into the second parlor. The first parlor and third bedroom remained empty throughout our residence.

Cushions followed next, three per trip, tied together with clothesline so none tumbled off the wagon. I struggled against every gust of wind to hold in place a painter's drop cloth draped over them to keep them dry as the snow fell in big, wet flakes.

Our bed frame, then the bedspring and mattress, each a separate trip, supported on the wagon by the two-by-fours, followed the same route, the balky drop-cloth tucked around them, too. It took my close attention to keep the wind from whipping it away. The frames of the two bedroom chests of drawers and the battered one from the closet followed — three more trips. Next, drawers were stacked on the wagon, two or three per trip, for several more trips. Radio, floor lamp, lamp table and lamps were all carted down the stairs and trundled down the street in turn, as well as our kitchen table upside down on the wagon. Finally, with two kitchen chairs at a time, we made the last two trips.

December's early darkness fell before we finished moving everything from the little apartment to the capacious flat. By then, our mothers had put most of our things in place and made up our bed while also caring for Gail. We all trekked down the block to Bill's mother's house, where we gratefully devoured a hearty stew she tended all afternoon with repeated trips back and forth to check on it while it simmered away in her kitchen.

After dinner, my parents left for the suburbs. Bill and I, with Gail in her carriage, walked past our emptied first apartment for our initial night at the new abode. As we passed, I looked up at the now-bare upstairs windows of our first home. They looked so forlorn I felt a stab of regret and a twinge of guilt at leaving it, but I knew it was not a safe residence for our baby.

A friend called from the front porch of her upstairs flat, "Hey! Do you guys want to come on over to celebrate New Year's Eve with us? Some of the neighbors will be here. You can bring the baby with you." We thanked her, but had to tell her we were too tired to stay up that late.

Lifting Gail's carriage up the porch steps and through the front door, we parked it in the empty front parlor, pulled off some of the blankets and left the baby to slumber on. Bill and I fell into bed and were asleep the instant our heads touched the pillows. There was no new-married love that night. I don't recall if we even took time to kiss.

I woke to hear church bells ringing and car horns blaring. "It must be midnight," I thought. I shook Bill to tell him, "Happy New Year, Darling!" He stirred, gave me a sleepy kiss, mumbled "Happy New Year, Sweetheart," and was instantly asleep again. That was the extent of our second married New Year's Eve celebration.

THE CHANGELING LANDLADY

An immediate blessing shortly before we moved was that Gail finally reached the stage of infant maturity where her stomach no longer rebelled. She began, almost overnight, to sleep peacefully between feedings. What a relief! Bill and I actually slept nights, too, except for those recurrent four-hour feedings. Gail, almost miraculously, became a much happier baby and we were better rested parents.

We hovered over her, friends dropped in to admire her. My parents, grandmother, aunts and uncles all came to see her. Bill's mother found some excuse to bring her to our apartment and then our flat on a daily basis. After those months of colic were over, we really enjoyed our darling girl.

When we first looked at the empty flat down the block from our apartment, the landlady averred with a smile that she "just loved" babies and young couples like us. She said she couldn't *wait* to watch Gail growing up! The fact that the flat was affordable, empty and immediately available despite the continuing scarcity of rental units gave us no pause in our eagerness to find a safe living arrangement. It should have.

After we moved in, our landlady was impossible to please. Within a week-and-a-half, she demanded we wear carpet slippers indoors, insisting she and her father were greatly disturbed by the sound of our footsteps on the floor of the flat below them. She then complained that Gail's crying kept her father awake. (She should have heard it earlier!)

By the end of our second week, the landlady banged a hammer on the pipes under her kitchen sink the moment Gail started to fuss. The noise reverberating through the building terrified Gail, who — naturally — cried all the harder. There were frequent loud slammings of doors upstairs in response to any slight sounds we made. How all that failed to disturb our landlady's father, we never asked.

The banging and slamming increased apace with the landlady's complaints. We were not to play a radio after 7:00 p.m. Intimidated, if we actually did listen to the weather report for the next day, we played it so softly we sat with our ears glued to the front of the speaker. We were not to speak above a whisper after dinner. We really tried, but Gail did not know how to whisper when her stomach required sustenance.

It was demanded that I not bump the kitchen sink or faucet with the dishes, pots or pans when I washed up after meals since "it disturbs my father." I washed up with the greatest of care. But no matter how I tried, pots placed on a porcelain drain board inevitably made at least a small "clink," always followed instantly by banging on the upstairs pipes. I wondered if the landlady knelt with her ear to the floor all day and evening breathlessly awaiting an excuse to wield her hammer.

One night, when I ran to warm Gail's bottle at 8:00 p.m., there was a different sound. That time the landlady's broom handle beat a furious staccato on our ceiling, followed closely by her presence at our back door, pounding and screaming for us to open up immediately! She ordered that henceforth we all retire for the night by 7:00 p.m. so as not keep her father up too late. Bill had to study late into the evenings, but we really did tiptoe and whisper as quietly as possible for her.

After we had been living there only a couple of months, the landlady rapped loudly on our door to demand hysterically that we find another place to live! Bill pointed out to her that we held a one-year lease and could not afford to lose our deposit. She screamed that she could not stand our "din" any longer, so would release us from the contract and return our deposit if we would — "*Please* GOD!" — move out quickly. Elated at the prospect of freedom from our haranguing landlady, we began searching for a new place to reside ... but all the rents listed in the newspaper were far too high for our budget.

YOU COULD ALWAYS GO TO <u>MY</u> MOTHER

I was never as patient as Bill. Under daily pressure from our landlady, my temper was strained. Ready to leave for school one morning, Bill mildly said something I construed as criticism. I responded angrily. He had been cuddling Gail before leaving for the day when I erupted. Bill tried to smooth it over, but nothing he said calmed me down. Angry at the landlady, I was itching for a fight, ready to do battle over anything!

After some conciliatory comments from Bill, which only added kindling to my fire, I blurted, "Alright! That's enough! This was a terrible mistake. We should never have gotten married in the first place!" Snatching Gail abruptly from Bill's arms, I added, "I'm going to take Gail and leave! And don't you try to stop me!" Gail began to cry, frightened by my sudden action. The plumbing resounded from the landlady's hammer. I stopped in the middle of the kitchen to pat the baby's back. Bill, startled into silence, thought quietly for a few seconds. Then, taking a deep breath, he said, in as reasonable a tone of voice as he could muster, "Well, you could do that. But remember that your mother told you after our wedding to visit often but never to come back home after we'd had an argument." I caught my breath, reminded of that truth.

"Of course, you could always go to *my* mother's," Bill added thoughtfully. "She'd certainly take you in." He waited a long moment before adding, "But I don't know how much good that would do you since I'd have to go there, too. I couldn't stay here all alone."

I knew I was being unreasonable. The volcano began to cool. Lava close to the surface subsided. Tears filled my eyes. Bill stood up, walked to where I stood to gently rub Gail's back. I looked up at him. I didn't know what to say. Gail was screaming in my ear. "Anyway," he added, putting his arms around both the baby and me, "I'd *want* to go there, too, because I love you."

I leaned my head on his shoulder. He patted my back, then took Gail from my arms. Comforted, she stopped crying. Bill gently put her down in her basket. She didn't cry. I did. Bill came back, wrapped me in his arms and said, "I don't EVER want to live anywhere you aren't." I cried harder, grateful to be secure in his love. Finally, hiccupping and sniffling, I ran down. "Do you think you'll be okay if I leave for school now?" Bill asked. I nodded. "I'm sorry — " I began. He silenced me with a kiss, hugged me tightly once more, went to take another look at Gail, came back to give me another hug, then left. I never, ever thought of leaving Bill again! He was my love and my anchor. He was such a reasonable man.

It was that very day, when Gail awakened for her next bottle, that I heard loud rapping on our back door. I recognized the sound. Warily, with Gail in my arms, I answered the summons. The landlady threw into the door a scattering of torn paper. "THERE!" she screamed. "There's your LEASE! Now you don't *have* one! You can GO! — As soon as you tell me you're leaving, I'll give you back your deposit. Just GO! GET OUT!" Of course, Gail began to cry at the shouting. The landlady turned on her heel and stamped up the stairs. Shakily, I closed the door and patted Gail's back till she calmed.

When the baby was again asleep in her basket, I scooped up the torn papers and stuck them together with tape to be sure they were actually our destroyed lease. I showed Bill the patched-up contract when he arrived home for dinner. "We really have to get out of here soon," he said. "She's getting nuttier by the day and I hate to leave you here alone to deal with her."

But our search for another apartment was discouraging; nothing advertised was affordable. At Mom Keeber's suggestion, clutching at straws, we posted notices on bulletin boards at the grocery, the hardware store and at church.

COULD WE REALLY <u>DO</u> THAT?

In just a couple of days, we were surprised by a visit from a parishioner who lived a few short blocks away. He didn't have anything to rent to us; instead, he had a three-bedroom fixer-upper house he hoped to sell. He and his wife were from the south. After one winter in Buffalo, they wanted nothing other than to depart the city forever to return home to "the hollers" where they had grown up. We thought the price named for the house might actually be affordable on Bill's G. I. student stipend of $115 per month!

We asked at a local savings and loan what deposit and monthly payment would be required. We learned that, since Bill was a veteran, we could buy the house with only 10% down and mortgage payments less than our rent!

Satisfied we could fund the purchase, we visited the house again, assessed its condition, thought with some qualms about all the labor it would take to make it satisfactory. But we were young and energetic so, after serious consideration based on our experience renovating our first apartment, we decided we could do the work ourselves. We took Gail to her grandma's, then went to present our formal offer. It was immediately accepted: $3,000 for the house! (At that time, very, very small new homes sold for about $12,000.)

Euphoric, we walked hand in hand back to Bill's mom's to pick up Gail. But then the inevitable doubts and afterthoughts nibbled at our enthusiasm. Breathless at our own audacity, we exclaimed to each other, "Wow! Three *thousand* dollars!" "Do you think we'll *ever* be able to pay off that much money?"

Nevertheless, faced with the choice of debt or crazy landlady, we immediately started proceedings to obtain a G.I. loan. We made plans to move in as quickly as we could close on the purchase, planning to work on redoing one room at a time in the evenings after Gail was asleep. Bill expected to finish studying after I went to bed to be able to wake with Gail for her night feedings. We knew it would take a long time to strip off old wallpaper, paint woodwork, make the whole house fresh and new. It was daunting, but the prospect of "fluffing and buffing" a home of our own was alluring. Especially enticing was the thought of escaping our impossible-to-please landlady!

THE DAY THE CEILING FELL

"Kin ah come in and talk to you an' the mister, Ma'am?"

It was about 7:30 on Friday morning, a week and three days before our scheduled closing date. We were counting down the *seconds* till moving day!

Bill was just finishing his morning coffee when the doorbell rang. Wondering who could be there at such an early hour, I opened the door to see the seller of "our" house, standing outside with his cap in his hand. Albert Hawkins and his wife, Letitia-Louise, were the couple who had agreed to sell us their century-old, fixer-upper house which would allow us to escape our difficult landlady.

Worried, I ushered him into the kitchen and offered him a cup of coffee. — We had given our landlady notice; new renters were waiting to move in on schedule. What if there was a problem with the sale of the house *now*? — Al took a long, slow swallow of coffee. He looked up at Bill, then away quickly. I could see Bill's tension-level rising, too.

"Yuh know how my wife Letty-Lou? ... she don' move very fast?" Al began. We both nodded. Al gulped. We were becoming more concerned by the second. "Well, this here mornin' – " He cleared his throat. Bill's and my eyes were glued on him, which appeared to make him all the more nervous. "This mornin'..." then there was another moment of silence.

He finally gathered his courage to rush through his next sentence like a runaway freight train. Breathlessly, he blurted, "This-mornin'-I-was-drinkin'-my-coffee-after-breakfast-an'-alla-sudden, outta-the-corner-a'-my-eye, I-saw-Letty-Lou-git-up-and-RUN! … fer the dinin' room doorway!" With his rush of words ended, he looked at us round-eyed, seemingly astonished even in retrospect. Bill and I couldn't imagine what Letty-Lou running for the dining room doorway had to do with us. We waited nervously. "And *then* the ceilin' hit me," finished Al.

"The CEILING?" Bill and I echoed in unison.

"Yup," said Al, looking a bit more comfortable now he had gotten it out. "Letty-Lou looked up from her breakfast and seen that plaster start to fall, an' she was so concentrated on gittin outta there that she didn't think to tell me about it. Whaddaya thinka *that*!?" he asked. Bill and I had no answer. We just stared at Al and wondered what was coming next.

Al resumed his worried frown, recalling the most important reason for his early-day visit. "I was hopin' this would'n stop y'all from buyin' the house. I called inta work and tol' my boss I hadda come talk to you about it right away. I already give my notice, so I don't know what Letty-Lou and me'll do if you don' go ahead an' buy it. Letty-Lou jis has her heart set on leavin' here for Kentucky next week. She's back at the house now, cryin' her eyes out with worryin'!" After his great effort to confess the problem to us, Al sort of sank into himself, appearing to shrink about three shirt sizes.

We were all in a bind. Al had given notice at work and would have no job in another week. We had given notice to our landlady and would have no home just after the week was out. None of us said a word for a moment. Bill set down his coffee cup with a sharp clink. "Al," he said, "I think you and I should walk over there and see what it looks like." With that, he pushed back his chair and stood up. Bill strode toward the door, Al right behind him. From the front window, I watched the two men descend the front steps and turn toward the corner. Gail awakened, crying for her bottle. The flat resounded with the sound of the landlady hammering on the pipes.

BILL'S PLAN

Bill was gone a long time. When he came back, he had a determined set to his jaw. "Bea," he said, "It's an awful mess over there. That ancient plaster just lost its grip on the lath and fell down all over everything. I'm not surprised Letty-Lou ran for her life when it started to come down! There's almost nothing left up there. There are plaster chunks and dust all over everything."

"What do you think we can do?" I asked him. "The first problem, right now," he told me, "isn't the plaster. It's that I don't know if the bank will give us the mortgage once they know about it."

I gasped in dismay. Bill reminded me, "After all, when they couldn't get FHA approval on the house with that barely-noticeable sag in the porch roof, they allowed us to contract with your uncle's building company to shore it up with new posts right after the closing. They accepted his cash bond to guarantee the work will be finished properly in a timely manner, and even agreed to accept our receipt from paying his $300 charge when the work is done as our delayed 10 percent down payment. They went *way* out on a limb to do that! … But I don't know if they'll be able to swallow this added problem." I stared at him wordlessly. "We'll just have to go over there and talk to them about it right away," Bill said.

Seeing my worried frown, he continued. "I stopped at Mom's on the way back, and she said we can stay at her house when we have to move out of here. She'll give the three of us her room and she'll move up to my old attic room. But the important thing right now is that we need to see if the bank will agree to my plan." "*What* plan?" I asked.

Bill explained. "Al and I talked it over. It'll be a whole lot of work to clean up that plaster, but I think we can all do it together. Mom said she could watch Gail full time so we can spend all the time we need on it. Letty-Lou moves too slowly to help; she'd just get in the way. But Al said he'd stop work immediately, after he goes in for his last paycheck this morning. The school is giving us vets a lot of leeway on attendance, so I can take off a week or so from school. I'll need to explain the problem to my advisor first, but I'm sure he'll allow me to catch up later." "But the closing is only a little over a week away! Do you think we can get a new ceiling put up in time?" I asked.

"No, but Al and I think that if we three all work really hard at cleaning up the plaster pieces and getting it swept out as fast as we can, we can make it look decent for a walk-through before the scheduled closing date. If the bank will agree to another cash bond to guarantee we'll do the job right, I can put up an acoustic tile ceiling *after* that. Mom said she could loan us money for the bond. She's coming over here to mind Gail; she'll be here any minute. You go put on overalls and a work shirt so you'll look as workmanlike as possible. Between us, maybe we can convince the banker to bet on us."

As I stood there digesting what Bill said, he reiterated, "We need to go talk to the banker. *Today! Right now!*" Just then, my mother-in-law arrived. I handed her the baby and dashed upstairs to change out of my housedress.

THE BANK

It was not one of your modern-day mega-banks. It was just a small neighborhood savings and loan. The current president, son of the late founder, was probably in his mid-60s. His son, the bank manager, was being groomed to assume the presidency when his father retired.

We approached the teller's window. "May we please speak to the manager about our mortgage?" Bill asked in a calm, business-like way. "We're scheduled to close next week." The teller shut her window and disappeared, then the manager stepped out to invite us into the smaller of the two offices.

Bill detailed the problem. He said he didn't think the ceiling could be put up before the scheduled closing date, but he expected to have it all ready for installation by then. He explained about Al's job and our apartment, and offered to put up a bond to guarantee the work would be properly completed in an acceptable amount of time, if we could just close on schedule.

Mr. Snyder looked at us thoughtfully. He leaned back and tented his fingers over his stomach. He looked at Bill with a small frown. "Because you're a veteran, we made an unconventional arrangement with you earlier regarding that porch roof," he said in what seemed to be an accusatory tone. Before Bill could reply, he asked, "Do you realize you would be working on a house you don't even own?" "Yes, Sir, I do," answered Bill. "But it looks to me like the only way we can get that house cleaned up in time for a walk-through. If we can have it all ready for the tiles to be installed by then, I was hoping you could still approve the mortgage." Before Mr. Snyder could say anything else, Bill added quickly, "Of course, we'd put up a bond to guarantee satisfactory completion of the job."

Mr. Snyder's brow furrowed. There was a long silence as he considered Bill's words. The interlaced fingers over his stomach moved up and down with each slow breath. We waited nervously. "I'd like to discuss this with my father," was his eventual response. He got up and left us to wait and worry.

Both Mr. Snyders returned. The older Mr. Snyder pulled a chair over so he could sit near Bill, who turned to face him. "All right, Son," he said, looking piercingly into Bill's eyes. "I want to hear this proposal you've put before us!" Bill took a deep breath and repeated his earlier speech to the bank manager. The president leaned back and looked at Bill thoughtfully. "Well, Mr. Keeber," said Mr. Snyder, Sr., "that's one of the most innovative proposals I've heard in a long time!" He leaned back and tented his fingers over his stomach, too, rubbing his thumbs together, looking up at the ceiling as if he'd find his response there. He was quiet for several long moments. We barely breathed, waiting.

Finally, he looked piercingly at Bill, then me, and said, "By God, let's go see this house together! I'll get my hat." He left the room, reappearing in a moment with his hat on his head. "Let's go!" he said, turning toward the door. Forgetting to even bid the manager goodbye, we jumped up and followed him. Together, we three walked the four blocks to the house.

Bill rang the doorbell. Letty-Lou, her face red and tear-stained, opened it. "Oh!" she said, "I'll git Al!" She turned away, just a bit less slowly than normal. "A-a-al?" we could hear her call. "Them Keeber folks is here, and they got somebody important-lookin' with 'em!" Al came to the door in dust-covered overalls. Bill explained that Mr. Snyder was the president of the bank and he wanted to see the damage. Glancing nervously at the man in the hat, Al opened the door wide. We all trooped back to the kitchen. The room was a mist of white dust. Mr. Snyder took out a handkerchief to cover his nose and mouth.

"Explain to me how you are thinking of tackling this job, Mr. Keeber," demanded Mr. Snyder. Bill outlined how his mom would mind our baby, he would take off from school and Al would quit work immediately. The three of us would clean out the broken plaster, sweep and wash up dust till the room was ready for the new ceiling. Bill detailed how he would re-nail the lath to the rafters above to be sure they were tight, then would attach acoustic tiles to the newly-firmed lath. He added that he planned to cut wood molding for the edges where the ceiling and walls met, but noted that he had a saw and miter box set, so he could do that.

"Have you ever done this sort of job before?" Mr. Snyder asked. "No, Sir. But I can see how it should be done and I know I can do it. I did a lot of repairs at my Mom's house after my dad's stroke, so I'm sure it's not hard."

Mr. Snyder shook out his handkerchief, sneezed once and put it back to his face. "Hm-m-m," he said thoughtfully. "Can you post a bond sufficient to hire a contractor if you find you can't do the work?" "Yes, Sir," answered Bill. "But I'll do it. My mother will loan us the money for the bond. It would take us a lot longer to pay her back if we had to hire a workman." There was a long silence. Bill, Al and I tried to avoid looking nervously at one another while we awaited Mr. Snyder's determination. The silence seemed to go on forever.

Mr. Snyder squared his shoulders and took a deep breath. He appeared to have made a decision. "Alright! I admire your spunk, young man," declared the bank president. "You go ahead and get a written estimate for the job to be done professionally and post a bond with us in that amount. If you three can have this room all cleaned up and ready for the ceiling to be installed, with the tiles purchased and here on hand by the time of the walk-through, I'll approve your mortgage and we'll close on time!"

He then turned to Al. "Sir, these young people are willing to put in their time and effort on this house which still belongs to you. I expect you to treat them fairly and work right along with them. I believe this is for your benefit as much as theirs since I understand you would like to move out of town right after the closing date." "Yes*sir*!" Al responded smartly. "I know it'll help me and Letty-Lou, so Ah'll work as hard as Ah kin with 'em!"

Mr. Snyder turned and reached for Bill's hand. They shook solemnly. "I've always believed good people could do business together on a handshake," said Mr. Snyder. "Now don't you disappoint me!" All three of us responded. "No sir, we won't do that!"

NUMBER 10 WAVERLEY STREET

Letty-Lou moved out of the house to stay at her cousin's nearby. I wheeled Gail and all her gear to her grandma's while Bill took a bus to and from the university to talk to his advisor. Before Bill and I arrived to start work, Al found a friend to help him shove everything movable from the kitchen to the dining room. He tacked a cloth over the dining room doorway.

Al slept at the house. Early each morning Letty-Lou brought him breakfast, coffee, and a sandwich from her cousin's before we arrived. I packed sandwiches and a thermos of tea for us each day. Late each afternoon, Bill's mother came to the house with Gail in her carriage, a box of warm food balanced on the hood. Bill, Al and I stopped only long enough to gulp down the meal and quickly return to work. Al worked with us as late each night as we could stay awake and on the job.

We had all the fallen plaster chunks out in a couple of day. We knocked down what little still clung to the lath. Bill swept the ceiling with a broom. Then he carried his mother's upright vacuum to the top of a ladder. I climbed up behind him, reaching past him to steady the vacuum in place while he used the hose attachment to clean the lath. We misted the dusty walls and floor with water-filled Windex bottles and swept them with dustcloth-covered brooms — over and over and over. Each time, dust roiled the air as soon as the water evaporated, but less and less as time went on.

It was Day Four when we could finally start washing the walls and floor. Pails of warm water thickened with plaster residue time and time again. At last, the rinse water from the walls appeared clean after midnight Saturday but dust from the floor still whitened the soles of our shoes. We had one more day, only half the weekend, before the walk-through on Monday morning. We went home to sleep for a few short hours. We hadn't even started packing to move out in time for the new tenants to occupy the flat on Tuesday morning.

Early Sunday, we hurried through breakfast. Mom arrived with Gail in the carriage to begin boxing up our belongings for the move. Bill and I left her working there when we returned to the house to begin washing the floor. I rinsed it again and again and *again*, as much with tears of exhaustion as tap water. It was about 2 a.m. when we finally decided there was no more plaster dust to be found anywhere.

Bill and Al brought in the boxes of acoustic tiles from the shed where they had been stored since they bought them from Sears two days earlier. They piled them up neatly in the corner. Bill and Al slapped each other's backs. Bill hugged me. Al went upstairs to bed and Bill and I walked to our flat, where we set the alarm for 6 a.m.

When it went off on Monday morning, we groggily opened our eyes to its pealing … and the landlady's furious hammering. I hurried to make breakfast while Bill bathed and dressed. Then he washed the dishes while I bathed and dressed. We wore work clothes, but clean ones, not plaster-crusted overalls like those we'd been in all week.

Mr. Snyder, Sr., arrived at the house promptly at 9:00 a.m. Al, Bill and I were ready and waiting for him. We all walked through the house. Letty-Lou had been there several times cleaning house while we worked in the kitchen. She may have been slow but she was thorough. The rest of the house sparkled.

Mr. Snyder looked at everything, starting with the clean living room, dining room, and first floor bedroom. He checked out the bathroom, pulling the chain on the overhead tank to loudly flush the toilet, turning the old claw-foot bathtub's faucets on and off, looking beneath to ascertain there were no leaks. He repeated those actions at the sink. Turning to the upstairs bedrooms, he even looked under Al's bed and found no dust; Letty-Lou had seen to that. He finally took a deep breath, squared his shoulders, and headed toward the kitchen as if he were loath to face it.

His mouth fell open. He looked up at the clean, bare lath on the ceiling. His eyes studied all four walls. He ran the palm of his hand down one and seemed surprised to find no dust on it. He licked his finger, bent down, ran it over the linoleum floor, stood up straight and examined the result. Turning to the three of us, he said emphatically, "I always DID believe in doing business on a handshake! You've done a fine job. I'll see you all at one this afternoon to sign the papers. Congratulations! You are hard-working young people."

At that, he turned on his heel and walked out the kitchen door to return to the Savings and Loan. We rushed to the front windows to see him turn onto the front sidewalk. He was whistling! We watched till he turned the corner. Then we erupted in cheers, high-fives, backslapping and laughter! Bill hugged me tightly.

We were actually going to be the owners — *that day!* — of our own house at 10 Waverley Street. We still had hours of work left to put up the ceiling tiles. Bill would work up on the ladder evenings, with me at the bottom of it, handing him one tile after another to speed up the job. But in just a few more days, we would have a brand-new kitchen ceiling in our own first house and Al and Letty-Lou would be happily settled back home in Kentucky.

Our move was hectic. After the closing, we vacated our flat in just a few hours. My dad and mother left work early to help pack up the last minute things. When that was finished, they went home, Mother complaining of a splitting headache from the landlady's frequent hammering! Bob showed up with his milk truck so he and Bill could move our stove, refrigerator and furniture. When they arrived with those, Al jumped in to help carry the refrigerator and stove into the kitchen. Somehow, with Bob's unflagging help, we moved everything out of the flat and into the house after the closing. As we carried things in, we kept passing Al and his friend moving his and Letty-Lou's belongings out to the rented truck Al planned to drive south to his wife's parents' place. It was all done by midnight. Our belongings were so jumbled together it took me months to actually find everything again!

Despite the late hour, we knocked on her door, demanded and received our deposit back from the landlady once the flat was emptied.

Bill started nailing lath first thing the next morning and went back to school on Wednesday. After spending the better part of each evening putting up tiles, he had to sit up very late studying to catch up.

Bill, Gail, and I did stay with Bill's mom, since, after the ceiling was up, we went ahead and stripped 18 layers of wallpaper from the kitchen walls and 21 from the rest of the house. We re-covered them with pretty new wallpaper, buying large double rolls for 15 cents each at a local outlet store.

Before Bill put up the new wall covering, we rented a large, commercial sander for me to clean layers of scratched brown paint from the floors. When I turned it on, I shrieked in alarm as it lurched around the room with me flying behind it like a kite! Bill raced into the room to rescue me and made quick work, himself, of sanding with the big machine. I stained and varnished the floor in one room while

Bill wallpapered in another one, then we switched locales. We both re-painted scarred woodwork.

My uncle quickly shored up the porch roof. We paid him our $300 and he gave us his receipt, which was to serve as our G.I. loan's official delayed down payment. He then surprised us by returning $100 in cash to us, saying it had taken him less time to finish the job than he expected, adding, " — and you don't need to mention this to the bank!" He also checked out the new ceiling for which he had provided the required professional job estimate, telling Bill approvingly, "I couldn't have done it better myself!"

Mr. Snyder, Sr. came over to inspect that and the porch roof. He approved both jobs and accepted our $300 receipt from Uncle Dave in lieu of our down payment. He pulled from his pocket two checks to refund the bonds. We immediately signed over one check to Bill's mom and the other to my uncle. Mom K helped me hang curtains. Together, we put away food and dishes in the pantry. Our linens went into the battered old chest now residing in the closet between the two upstairs bedrooms. The house was clean, with newly-painted woodwork, freshly-papered walls, neatly-curtained windows and warmly glowing wood floors when Bill, Gail and I moved into it about four weeks after the closing. We never expected to have it so nicely completed so soon. It was only possible because we stayed at Bill's mom's till it was done.

Our little house had only one bathroom, upstairs on the second floor. Despite the location of the house in winter-frozen Buffalo, N.Y., there was no central heat, only an electric radiant heater in the bathroom and a noisy, roaring old oil stove in the dining room. Open grates in the dining room and living room ceilings allowed a modicum of heat to rise into the perpetually-chilly upstairs bedrooms. But with new wallpaper, beautifully finished wood floors and frilly sheer curtains, it was a palace to us!

With the refund my uncle gave us, our house actually cost us $2,900 plus half the price of the ceiling tiles Bill and Al purchased together. I don't recall their cost, but it wasn't much. Our mortgage payment, in 1950, was $29 per month, including interest, principal, tax escrow and homeowner's insurance. That astonishingly low payment made it possible for Bill to stay in college to persevere on toward his Ph.D. When we sold that little house, we made a profit of $2,600, which provided the down payment and closing costs on our next house purchase in 1956. That price tag, however, was $21,500.

But before that time, our cozy little first house in Cold Spring saw a lot of living. With un-insulated walls, cold nights and warm love, our family expanded with the arrivals of three more children.

A MOUSE IN THE PANTRY!

"BILL! A mouse! A MOUSE!!! A <u>MOUSE!!!</u>" I wasn't frightened. I was furious!

In July, we moved in after painting, wallpapering and lining pantry shelves with fresh newspaper. Everything was spanking clean. In late September, I found field mouse droppings on the shelves. This invasion was not to be tolerated! I moved all the foodstuffs, pots and pans to the drop-down counter Bill built over the laundry tubs, denuded the shelves of their newspaper liners, cleaned and scrubbed from top to bottom.

That evening, with a flashlight, Bill searched out the small hole providing the offending creature's entry. In the garbage, he found an empty tomato juice can. I washed it thoroughly, then Bill cut it open with tinsnips, hammered it flat on the cement sidewalk. When he brought it back indoors, he filled the tiny hole with spackle and nailed the flattened can over it. I retrieved from a fruit cellar shelf the remnants of the wallpaper we had recently used so Bill could paper over the offensively bright metal. The pantry looked snug and clean again with its neat, flower-bedecked wallpaper.

Barely a week later I saw new mouse droppings on a pantry shelf. If I could have wrung that mouse's neck, I would have done so with fervor! Once again, I removed all the contents of the pantry. Bill found another can to hammer flat, nailed it over a new hole, patch-papered over the can. That time, he went outdoors to sprinkle mouse poison at the base of the wall under the window. I dressed the shelves with fresh newspapers and put back all that belonged on them.

Teeth clenched, we went through that same routine a week-and-a-half after that. That time, Bill inched through the spidery crawl space to sprinkle poison on the ground just inside the foundation wall beneath that window.

Then, just days later, I went down to the kitchen in the middle of the night to heat a bottle for Gail — and there was a tiny, tiny mouse calmly sitting on the kitchen floor, bits of crumbs clinging to his whiskers. I saw red! How *dare* he? How did he get in again? I morphed into a war machine, bent only on death to the intruder.

Yelling for Bill, I ran to the hook in the pantry where I kept my broom. The mouse watched me as if I were an exhibit at the zoo. I raised the broom high over my head; luckily the ceilings in that old house were high. With a banzai whoop, I swung the broom down fiercely — only to hit bare linoleum. The mouse had prudently scampered beneath the refrigerator to assess his next move in this new game. Then he stuck out his nose and risked a teasing scamper across the kitchen.

The broom whizzed audibly through the air while I screeched imprecations at the intruder, belatedly drawing Bill out of bed and down the stairs. The mouse had it down perfectly. I thought for sure I had him dead to rights, but he timed his race to safety under the stove with a mini-second to spare.

"Bill, get him *out* of there!" I screamed in frustration. Bill found a yardstick, poked it under the stove and flushed out the mouse, by that time possibly a mite alarmed. The mouse bolted for the refrigerator. As he raced rapidly past me, I raised the broom, loosed my war-whoop, and brought the broom down hard — once again on bare linoleum. The mouse passed me before the broom landed.

Bill poked the yardstick vigorously under the refrigerator until the mouse made a dash for the stove again. Shrieking loudly, I did the broom thing once more to no avail. On hands and knees, Bill scurried back to the stove, but the mouse tired of the game. Instead of dashing for the refrigerator once more, the little culprit raced between Bill's knees, heading for the narrow space between the closed dining room door and the floor. Fearing I would lose my prey, I shoved the broom across the floor like a snowplow as fast as I could run. Just as the mouse made it to the opening, the broom connected. Little hind feet splayed wide. There was a high-pitched "E-E-E-e-e-E-E-E-E" from the mouse. But still he disappeared beneath the door! I wrenched the door open, but there was no sign of my prey.

Turning back to the kitchen, I saw Bill on the kitchen floor, his knees drawn up, clutching his stomach, laughing so hard his punctuating breaths sounded like whooping cough. Enraged at losing my troublesome prey, and now further enraged at Bill for *laughing*, I threw the broom to the floor, declaring, "YOU warm the bottle and tend to Gail! I'M going to bed!" As I stamped up the stairs, I could hear Bill still choking with amusement as he opened the refrigerator.

Slowly waking in the morning, memories of the night's antics began to sift into my consciousness. I turned to see Bill sleeping peacefully beside me — and felt no murderous impulses. I giggled at the recollection of my Banzai attacks. Bill opened one eye. "Is it safe to say 'Good morning'?" he asked tentatively. I gave him a big kiss. "Yes!

You can say 'Good Morning,'" I declared. "But we have a big job to do on that darned pantry again." Bill groaned. It was Saturday morning and he hoped to sleep late. "But Gail's not awake yet, so we still we have time for some cuddling!" I told him cheerfully. Bill turned to me with anticipation and open arms. "That's more like it," he declared, "…a loverly way to start the day!" We didn't get up till Gail stirred a good hour later.

We repeated the pantry patching a fourth time, thoroughly discouraged, convinced it was only a holding action. But neither the mouse nor any of his friends or cousins ever reappeared. We surmised that, after he escaped, he told all and sundry to avoid that house at Number 10 because of the wild woman there with that killer broom!

DAVID WILLIAM

With my second pregnancy, I was excited to feel life when, suddenly — no movement. A day passed, then two more. There was definitely a change! Mother, Grandma and Mom K were sure the baby was lost. They wanted me to ask the doctor to end the pregnancy for my safety. "It doesn't look good for the success of the pregnancy," he admitted, "but it's best to let Mother Nature move at her own pace." His suggestion was, "Give it a little time and just take it easy." The grandmothers' worries had started me fretting, but I went along with Dr. Lechner's decision. Mom K took up residence on our couch to care for Gail — and as much of the housework as she could prevent me from doing.

But my family's worried comments — "Gail needs her mother! How could Bill raise a little girl if you weren't here?" — soon made me ill with apprehension. Dr. L decided he would gently try to encourage natural labor — no irresistible drugs, just castor oil. Nothing happened, except that the castor oil did what castor oil had done for generations. I experienced a few contractions along with the diarrhea and cramps it caused, but labor did not begin when the castor oil's influence ceased. Dr. L adamantly refused to move ahead with anything more insistent than the laxative. I had had enough of castor oil. We were at an impasse.

Then I felt movement again! Not just once, but several times! Mother insisted I go to *her* doctor immediately before consulting Dr. Lechner. Dr. Schmidt was a well-respected obstetrician before he partially retired to general practice when the hours of his preferred specialty threatened his health. He determined there was indeed movement — it was not just gas! He also discovered a "dead spot," as he described it, where he could hear nothing. He concluded that the sac in which the baby resided had partially pulled away from its attachment to the uterus, causing the lack of sound in that area. He thought that was worrisome, and suggested I continue to utilize Mom K's help with Gail.

I went back to Dr. Lechner. His opinion matched Dr. Schmidt's. "Yes, there IS movement. The baby seems alright. I don't know what happened, but just be glad — and take it easy!" Mother, Grandma and Mom K were then convinced Dr. L knew his business, too. My own faith was restored when I realized that his refusal to give me anything other than castor oil — probably to salve my worries in the least harmful manner — had possibly saved our baby's life. I walked gently, as if I were carrying a box of fresh eggs home from the market!

I began to grow larger. There was definitely a baby in there! I cheered up, despite the nagging worry in the back of my mind that something might still be wrong, but the pregnancy continued as if nothing unusual had occurred. When Doctor Lechner heard a good heartbeat, he pronounced the pregnancy "on the tracks again." I was warned to do nothing overly strenuous, but I could resume daily housework and the care of Gail. Mom K returned to her own bed, but she dropped in daily on one excuse or another, and always stayed to do a few of the household chores.

At last, I reached term and labor began. Unlike Gail's delivery, this one was long but it wasn't painful; I breathed as taught in Dr. Read's book. Then labor ceased — no contractions, no discomfort, nothing. This new baby appeared to be in no hurry at all! The floor nurse sent me up to the hospital roof garden to walk — to encourage labor to recommence, she said. My feet hurt. I complained. The nurses encouraged me. Bill was sympathetic, but thought perhaps I ought to follow advice — after all, those nurses had been helping to usher babies into the world for a long time. I thought about the obstetrical nurse who could not believe Gail's delivery was painless. I wasn't so sure.

I walked and walked. My feet hurt and hurt some more. Finally, I rebelled. "I'm not walking another step!" I told Bill, who told Dr. L. "That's fine," he reassured us calmly. "I don't think anything will bring the baby 'til the baby is ready to arrive, anyway. The nurses think walking is a good idea, and it doesn't do any harm, but you have every right to just sit and wait." I did. After 24 hours without apparent labor, David finally decided to make his appearance. Bill had been with me in the labor room, on the roof garden for my time there, for the entire unproductive 24 hours when nothing was happening, but the hospital staunchly refused to allow him to enter the delivery room. I expected to watch David's arrival in the mirror as I had Gail's. But once David finally made up his mind, he decided he was in a hurry. I was barely into the delivery room when he emerged — before I even had time to glance at the mirror. I was disappointed to miss the show!

He was a big boy. He didn't complain about anything. I held him for a little while, but it didn't upset him at all when the nurse took him from me to the nursery. The doctor was still busy. He explained there was a copious afterbirth. He took a long time. Bill later told me he paced the fathers' waiting room once again positive something was wrong.

Bill was shown the baby as he was taken to the nursery for his bath. "He's the ugliest infant I've ever seen!" bewailed my husband when he saw me. Dr. L explained to us that the lengthy labor, non-labor, then strong labor caused temporary distortion to David's still-malleable face and head. Calmly, he told us that in a day or two, our son would be as handsome as Gail had been pretty. Bill worried. I worried. Dr. L was right. By the time I left the hospital days later, the nurses were exclaiming about our "future heartthrob" of a baby boy.

Bill was totally delighted with Gail, and now thrilled to have a son. David weighed in at just over eight pounds, compared to Gail's six. Before I left the hospital, I confessed to Dr. Lechner that I had seen Dr. Schmidt partway through the pregnancy. He was not offended. In fact, he contacted Dr. Schmidt so they could discuss their findings. They said it was a "very interesting case."

Their considered, joint opinion was that the pregnancy started with fraternal twins, whose gestations might have been launched at slightly different times — perhaps an evening and a morning. One grew more rapidly than the other, quickened earlier, and needed more sustenance. The doctors believed one twin was in an incompletely attached sac, which could not provide enough nourishment. That one could not survive. Since the environment in which he resided was sterile and a separate apartment from his brother's, there was no problem for the remaining fetus. In the ensuing months, the first baby was gradually reabsorbed into the amniotic fluid, leaving nothing to be identified but that unusually copious afterbirth. The doctors concluded that David was the single healthy survivor of fraternal twins.

I felt badly to think one twin had not survived, but I was also secretly and a bit guiltily relieved I didn't have two infants to care for along with Gail. How that twin theory would stand up to more modern obstetrics' understanding remains a question in my mind. I may indeed have lost one twin. I mourned for that baby, but was thrilled with the one I had.

Where Gail's first few months featured colic as her tiny stomach learned to cope with food, David arrived larger, hungry, prepared to do battle for his nourishment. He attacked his bottles as if they were enemies from whom he had to wrench his needs. Once satisfied by a gargantuan helping, he slept peacefully until his gauge again registered empty.

MOTHER CAME TO HELP

As the time for David's arrival neared, my mother felt guilty that Bill's mom had been the one to assist me after we had Gail. She firmly insisted she would take off work to help when I came home after David's birth.

Because of Mother's fragile health, she found office work easier than homemaking. Dad generally made no-nonsense British Army-style bacon, eggs and strong tea for breakfasts. Mother made tasty sandwiches for lunch. She assembled all sorts of creative combinations for my school lunches. By dinnertime, Mother was intimidated, disinterested or perhaps too tired. The results were usually unremarkable.

Earlier in my second pregnancy, Mum watched me run after Gail, noting that it's a good thing God gives babies to *young* people. She said just watching Gail run was enough to make her tired! However, Mother was an admirable, strong-willed woman who did her best to measure up to her own overly-high standards, which frequently resulted in her attempting more than her strength warranted. I couldn't think how to decline Mum's proffered help. I mentioned my concerns to Bill, who was also loath to offend her — so Mother came to help.

I came home from the hospital with David and a raging headache, which hung on for about three days. Allergies sometimes caused those. Mother was there already, nervously fluttering about. Bill left for as many of his day's classes he could still catch. Mom Keeber had stopped in to greet the new baby; she efficiently settled him into his basket while I headed straight to bed, blinds drawn against offending light.

When David awakened, Bill's mother was gone, so my mother brought the baby to me in bed. She stepped nervously around Gail, jumping like a pogo player trying to see her brother. Mum was clearly glad to escape to warm David's bottle. She returned, wearing a worried look. "I hope it's the right temperature," she ventured, handing it to me. Splashing a drop on my wrist, I proclaimed it fine, and popped it into the baby's mouth. Mother hovered indecisively for a moment, then offered to read a story to Gail, who left happily with her hand in her grandmother's.

After awhile, Mother took sleepy David from me to change him, but she looked so wary that I climbed out of bed despite my pounding temples and did the job myself. Relieved, Mother departed for the kitchen, saying she needed to start dinner.

After bringing David and me home from the hospital that morning, Bill went on to school. When he came home, his first stop, as usual, was the kitchen where he always sniffed appreciatively and lifted pot lids to peek at what was cooking. He made his normal kitchen detour, then came into the bedroom to see me. I opened my eyes to observe an uncharacteristic frown on his face.

"What's wrong?" I asked. "Your mother ... " then he hesitated. "Oh-oh, what did she do?" "It's what she's *doing*, "Bill told me. "She's boiling a sirloin steak in a full pot of water. She says she's making Swiss steak for dinner!"

Mother always approached cooking as if everything came alive and predatory and must be killed in the pot — and she did an admirable job of that. I groaned and started to push back the bedclothes. "No, no," Bill said. "Stay there. Maybe I can help." Given that Mother was unacquainted with salt, pepper, spices or condiments, even if Bill surreptitiously added a bay leaf and some salt to the unseasoned water, it was certainly too late in the game to make much difference.

The pale tan "Swiss steak" was fished out of its bath, placed on a platter with potatoes and carrots boiled in the same pot to a state almost beyond recognition. Bill brought a tray to my bedroom, his lips a straight, tight punctuation in his face. He raised his eyebrows at me as the only comment he was prepared to make, and exited. I chewed on the tasteless meat and swallowed the flavorless, cooked-to-mush vegetables, thanking Heaven that neither Mother nor Grandma ever ventured to teach me to cook. It was difficult learning from scratch after marriage, but Bill was patient, and with Mom K's tactful tutelage, I enjoyed learning to cook meals Bill loved.

I have no idea what Bill reported to his mother, but the next day, Mom Keeber showed up in mid-afternoon to coo at David and play a bit with Gail. Mother had taken to sighing loudly as she ran after her. Mom suggested that Mother must be tired by then. Mum readily agreed. Mom K suggested Mother take a bit of a rest and let *her* see to dinner that night. When Mum thanked her, Mom hurried to the kitchen, from which wonderful aromas soon wafted. I could smell onion, browning chicken, sage and other appetizing scents I enjoyed in anticipation.

By the time Bill arrived home, Mother looked more rested, Gail was happily playing under her gaze and the house had a tantalizing aroma. I decided to join the family for dinner instead of having a tray in the bedroom.

Bill's mother was serving up a hearty chicken stew, replete with noodles perfectly done, and a medley of cooked-just-right vegetables. There was a crisp salad ready and a tray of biscuits fresh from the oven. She must have brought over a jar of her home-canned cherries; I could smell a pie, too, which I spied cooling on the counter. Mother exclaimed over how good everything looked, and tucked in with enthusiasm. It wasn't that she didn't enjoy good cooking; she simply had no skill at it. To her credit, Mother *did* make delicious pineapple upside-down cake and tasty fruitcakes for the holidays. She baked a very good apple pie, too, with a wonderful flaky crust, a favorite of my father's.

The next day, Mother arrived a good couple of hours after my mother-in-law showed up. Bill's mother had Gail dressed, David changed, and both fed by the time Mum arrived.

Mom K suggested Gail might like to have a story read to her by my mother. She then efficiently put laundry into the washer, after which she and Mum sat in the living room chatting, with Gail playing at their feet. I was ordered by both of them to rest in bed and concentrate only on David all that day. Although my headache was improving, I was glad to comply.

I know Mother folded the laundry and read a story to Gail, but I don't know what else she may have done that day. Bill's mom made another delicious dinner, at which my father joined us. When it came time for Dad and Mother to leave, Mom K said, "You know, I really have nothing else to do with my time and I could help Bea without any trouble. It's a shame for you to let work pile up at the office when I could so easily be here."

Mother looked at Dad, a hopeful look of relief flooding her face. But then her face reflected concern. I knew she wondered if it would be desertion to return to the work she so much preferred. I added, still feeling a stubborn throb in my temples, "Mum, I really appreciate your help, but I feel so much better now. If Mom Keeber can come over for just a couple of days, I think it will be fine!" Dad said, "Well, Marge, that seems to say your help is redundant. Why don't you come to the office tomorrow? We certainly could use you there!" I knew that was true; Mother was so efficient in an office. She thanked Mom and agreed that if we really didn't need her, she would go back to helping Dad.

After they left, Mom and Bill washed up. Mom said I should rest and she'd put Gail to bed. Bill came into our bedroom with me, closing the door behind us. "*Yeah!*" he exclaimed, punching his fist into the air. I laughed at his elation and noted that Mum tried her best, but just wasn't very good with children or cooking. Bill smiled and added, "Well, she <u>did</u> try hard."

He went to bid his mother goodnight, then returned, saying, "I locked up. Why don't we have an early night?" I agreed. My head was still not feeling quite up to par. Settled in his arms, I slept like a baby. In the night, Bill warmed David's bottle and brought him to me in bed. We both sat up in bed watching his meal devoured with gusto. My headache had left the premises. We could see David would enjoy his food like his dad.

DORSEY, WAGNER AND CROSBY - FOR BABYSITTERS?

When David was three or four weeks old, I wheeled his basket to the dining room, parking it in front of the china cabinet so he could sleep while I dusted the living room.

I placed a small portable radio, tuned to the news broadcast, on an open shelf, volume up to hear it in the living room. When the news ended, a program of classical music was announced. I continued dusting, prepared to listen while I worked, but David started to fuss. The crying intensified by the mini-second. When David wanted his bottle, even as young as that, he wanted it right then and there!

When the music began, I could hear the first couple of bars filtered through David's outraged yells. But then David went silent. He even stopped moving, as if someone turned a switch! His fists, pumping as furiously as an apprentice pugilist, stilled in mid-air. I don't recall the selection, but I do remember it was a heroic Germanic one. David stilled, his ears working overtime. Astonished, I watched David actively listening till the lengthy piece neared its conclusion. I realized I needed to warm his bottle quickly!

As the last note died away, there was an intake of David's breath as he revved up to complain loudly of his empty midsection. I took the bottle from the warm water, tested the contents on my wrist while David's roars became more insistent. The next selection began — and there was instantaneous quiet. It was magic! I picked up the silent baby, walked into the living room, followed by Gail, who sat beside me watching her new brother. Rather than attacking his bottle forcibly to wrest every ounce from it, David nursed quietly, almost casually, listening to the music.

From then on, music calmed David under any circumstance. It wasn't just classical music; any music had the same effect, from the thunder of the German masters to Big Band Swing or Crosby's croon. Born with a "tin ear," I pounded through childhood piano lessons oblivious of sour notes. I did learn to discern wrong notes, but am an undiscriminating listener, enjoying the broad sounds of music rather than individual nuances. In contrast, Bill listened intently and analytically for every note, every instrument's contribution. I was amazed that David, so very young, showed clear evidence he had inherited Bill's concentrated focus on musical sounds.

When David graduated from infancy to competing with Gail for toys, battles became frequent, but music always calmed things instantly. Gail might be fractious, but David stopped responding to her as soon as music began.

David was two years, nine-and-a-half months old when John joined our ranks. David thereby graduated to "big boy" status, active, curious and into everything. Gail took over as "little mother," watching him, warning about things she knew were dangerous, calling me when he persisted. David was a tease. When he tired of Gail "minding" him, he goaded her by doing things he knew would upset her … until music captured his attention. More and more often, I called on my unusual babysitters — Dorsey, Wagner and Crosby — to keep peace.

THE NEW DISHWASHER

"Bill! Look at this. Sears is advertising a new sort of dishwasher. It's hydraulic — just water power. Look how inexpensive it is!"

When we first moved into our house, we bought an automatic washer so I didn't have to traipse over to Mom K's house with laundry. After the dryer came a year later, I no longer had to hang wash to dry on lines in the yard or attic. But dishwashing was the continuing bane of my life, a chore I hated with passion! After we had been in our house close to three years, I saw the advertisement when I paged through the newspaper at breakfast with Bill.

Just a short time earlier, Bill had unexpectedly become well practiced at plumbing. In anticipation of hot water at the turn of the tap for his morning shaves, he moved our old kitchen hot water heater down into the fruit cellar, where he installed an automatic thermostat on it. What luxury! No more waiting forever for hot water!

But then we found a puddle beneath the kitchen sink — the next connection up the line from the tight new ones in the fruit cellar. Bill's efforts to tighten the joint under the kitchen sink did not help, so he installed brand-new pipes and connections there. Then as I washed dishes, we heard drips beneath the laundry tubs *next* to the kitchen sink. As Bill made each repair, the next joint along the line leaked. Those pipes were so old that successive repairs precipitated sequential disasters. Bill ended up re-plumbing our entire house with new pipes and new, tightly sealed joints.

Feeling well qualified to install it, Bill decided I really needed that new dishwasher. He was sure his new plumbing would accommodate it. But a major alteration to our kitchen floor plan was necessary. All the walls were fully utilized by the refrigerator, washing machine, two laundry tubs, drain board, sink, stove, worktable, dryer, folding table, plus doorways to the shed, kitchen porch, dining room, stairway and pantry! The table, chairs and high chair occupied the center of the room.

Despite the labor involved, Bill felt I needed the dishwasher. He installed the range, new dishwasher, dryer and a small work counter all in a row down the center of the room — a peninsula facing the refrigerator, washer, laundry tubs and sink. Then he built a half-wall behind them to protect the backs of the appliances from small fingers. We moved the table, chairs and high chair to the window wall.

With the appliances newly positioned, the floor began to creak and sag alarmingly. The original 12" square hand-hewn beam in the fruit cellar was insufficient to bear the added weight! With jacks supporting the kitchen floor and appliances so they didn't end up in the fruit cellar, Bill cut out the old beam in 12" sections and inched a steel I-beam into its place. The substitution worked – no more creaks or sags! It was an ambitious undertaking — but Bill never did anything halfway, nor did he tire easily.

Mom K's opinion was that an automatic dishwasher was a total waste of money, since she could easily conquer a sink full of dishes in half the time a dishwasher took. But I was thrilled with my new wonder, which came complete with a small sample box of detergent. Having watched the model dishwasher loaded in the store, I didn't waste time reading the instructions.

As soon as Bill finished the installation, I enthusiastically filled the new appliance with dirty dishes and poured in the detergent. When it stopped, I took out sparkly-clean dishes. "Look, Bill! They're perfectly clean! Isn't that marvelous? What a work-saver!" Bill was pleased with the result of his efforts. Next I loaded the pots and pans waiting in the kitchen sink — I hated washing those! They all came out clean and shiny. "Bill, it even cleans pots and pans!" I washed the rest of the stacked dishes in the pantry. Then I brought the good china from the dining room and washed all of that. Last, I washed all the unused pots and pans in the house so everything would shine equally brightly.

I called Mom K that evening. "Mom, you should see it! All I do is load the dishes and pots and pans and they all come out sparkling!" She said she'd come over the next afternoon to see it in action. I saved the breakfast and lunch dishes to show her the worth of our new appliance.

When Mom arrived, I was so eager to show off my new wonder! But first, I made coffee and cut slices of the home-baked coffee cake Mom brought with her. After filling our plates and cups, the demonstration began. I loaded the dirty dishes and still found room for breakfast and lunch cookware. Surprised to see that the small sample box of detergent was empty, I poured laundry powder into the cup, closed the dishwasher and turned it on. Then I sat down to enjoy coffee and a visit with Mom, with the comforting sound of the dishwasher's swirling water in the background. As we chatted, Mom looked toward the dishwasher. Her coffee cup halted halfway to her lips. Her mouth opened. I turned to see what she was observing.

The lid of the dishwasher was slo-o-owly rising of its own volition. As we watched, it opened fully, then fell backward with a loud clatter. A white cloud of suds emerged and rapidly built to an alarming height. Jumping up, I raced around the peninsula to turn off the machine.

The mountain of suds continued to grow until the dishwasher basket gradually stopped circling. The foam stopped climbing, but didn't recede.

I scooped up a handful of dry suds — they were almost solid! I put my hand under the faucet, the foam grew again momentarily as the water fed it, then succumbed to the strength of the stream, slid off my palm to the drain where swirling water finally carried it away.

I turned to scoop more foam from the mound over the dishwasher. Mom walked over to look. It was going to take a long time to deplete that white mountain before I could even *find* the dishes inside the dishwasher. Mom fetched a two-quart pot from the pantry shelf. Scooping up foam, she put it under the faucet. Suds rose alarmingly, shrank, then slithered down the drain.

I found another pot. Without a word, Mom and I scooped up pots of foam, washing it down the drain. Mom never smiled. She just kept scooping and rinsing. For a change, I was speechless.

Eventually, we reached the dishes. Each one had to be rinsed under copious cold water till the stubborn suds disappeared. I handed dishes to Mom, who placed them under the stream of water and then into the drainer tray. Mom poured hot water over the cold, wet dishes in the drainer, while I brought a stack of dishtowels from the pantry. We hand-dried them, then began again.

Finally, carrying the clean dishes to the pantry, I noted that I'd have to call Sears to service the appliance. Mom reached for the instruction book I left on the counter the day before in my eagerness to try out the dishwasher. She flipped through a couple of pages, then commented mildly that it said the dishwasher needed a special non-sudsing detergent from Sears. She showed me the booklet. There it was — in capital letters: "DO NOT USE SUDSING DETERGENT."

Mom drove to Sears to buy me some of the special detergent. Before she returned, I hand-washed and dried our coffee cups and plates at the kitchen sink. My mother-in-law earned her crown in Heaven that day.

HOW ABOUT ANOTHER BABY?

When David was about two, Bill and I watched the children play. "He's not a baby anymore," I commented to Bill. "No," he agreed, "he doesn't even walk like a baby now." "I thought I'd have a little one to cuddle for a bit longer than this," I said ruefully.

"What would you think about starting another one?" Bill surprised me with his suggestion, since he tended to worry more about money than I did. Bill worked hard at part-time jobs to supplement his student stipend. I worked at being thrifty and saving what we had. I looked at him questioningly, but his cheerful leer indicated he meant what he said.

Bill surprised himself by thoroughly enjoying parenthood. Before the children were born, having no experience with siblings, neither of us had any concept of them as individuals, particularly *small* individuals. It came as a surprise to us when each one was born with a distinct personality, evident almost from Day One. We had assumed children in one family would be more or less carbon copies, but in male or female form.

Watching Gail and David develop was a daily delight as we noted the differences between their individual emerging characters. Gail was busily active, cheerful and affectionate. She stepped up early to take responsibility for her younger brother, her attention to his doings ever-present in her mind from his earliest entry into the family. It was almost as if she were born to be a parent and caregiver. David was independent, very active, too, but you could almost see gears turning in his head when he paused to quietly consider things. David was an instigator — devising all sorts of creative mischief. (Over the years, he managed to engineer an astonishing variety of "interesting" doings among his siblings and friends.) Bill and I both enjoyed watching their minds and curiosities develop. But I particularly enjoyed their cuddly baby stages, which turned out to be so fleeting.

Bill said, "Just think of it — no bothersome birth control! We could just take our time and make another baby." That sounded good to me. We had planned to wait seven or eight years for our first, but that was only the beginning of the era of mechanical birth control. When, despite our best efforts, I became pregnant for the first time, we simply tightened our belts, planned for me to work as long as practical, then stay home and be a full-time mother. When I became pregnant again, due to deliver only 22 months after Gail's arrival, we accepted that we were not in control of family planning despite those newfangled birth control methods, which promised much but failed to match their press.

We agreed it was a good thing for children to grow up with siblings close enough in age to play together. It did seem the right time for a new baby.

Bill and I loved to sleep "spoon-fashion." He'd pull me to him under the covers, drag my pillow close to his, tuck his arm beneath the pillow and around me, his hand warmly cupping one breast. He often told me he was glad I wasn't a "Busty Betsy" since he had a "perfect handful." During the night, one of us might roll over and break the embrace, but more often than not, I awakened cuddled close to Bill in the morning, his warm hand still gently caressing me.

If the children were quiet, Bill might kiss the back of my neck and questioningly squeeze my breast. I'd roll over and snuggle closer to him, feeling his response through my nightgown. It wouldn't take long for nightgown and pajamas to hit the floor as our libidos took over. Sometimes we made love before sleep and also on awakening.

But birth control was such a bother. When it became apparent we weren't just cuddling, I had to leave Bill's warm arms and our cozy bed to rush into the cold bathroom to insert a "ring," as we called the birth control method then most favored. I'd hurry back to bed to resume our lovemaking, but we both hated that chilling interruption.

The day Bill suggested we enlarge the family and I agreed, he was eager to make love without that bother. He helped me put the children to bed, as he often did. But instead of hitting his textbooks, he helped dry dishes and clean up the kitchen, then pulled the blinds and settled the house for the night even before it was fully dark.

We walked up the narrow stairs two-by-two, hip-to-hip, playfully nudging each other every few steps. Bill suggestively helped me undress, then quickly shed his own clothing, leaving it all in a heap on the floor; we had no interest in wasting time to hang things in the closet. We made passionate love till we rested, then we made love some more.

This business of making a new baby was going to be great! No more interruption just as things warmed up, no more cold bathroom, no return of my chilled body to temporarily dampen enthusiasm! Night after night, and frequent early mornings, with only a short, grudging intermission in the middle of the month, we allowed our libidos their heads with the intention of thoroughly enjoying this business of making another baby.

Then came the end of the month when I expected my period. I counted the standard 28 days. I was regular as clockwork. I decided I must have counted wrong until 29 days passed — 30 days — 31 days. I dreaded telling Bill that our plan for a long, passionate pre-baby period might be truncated. But Bill caught on quickly. He was counting days, too, expecting to be celibate through my menses.

"When is your period due?" Bill asked. "Well-l-l, actually I expected it four days ago," I admitted. "You're always on time, aren't you?" Bill asked. "For as long as I remember, except when Gail and David were on the way." "Do you think we connected right away — just like that?" Bill asked. "I don't know … but it looks possible," I admitted.

By the end of another week, there was no more guessing. "Who'd expect the arrow to hit the bull's eye first time out of the quiver?" Bill said wonderingly one evening. "Some people have to try for a couple of years to achieve pregnancy — I guess I'll just call you "Fertile Myrtle" from now on!" We laughed ruefully, but Bill was always a man who took life as it came and made the best of it, rarely feeling impelled to battle fate. He said, "Anyway, we have almost nine months of not bothering with birth control, don't we?" So we made the most of the next months.

JOHN WILLARD

John Willard arrived on May 16th, 1954. He took his time about it; it was a long, mild, unproductive labor for several hours. Bill was with me, but there was little for him to do … we just chatted and napped most of that time. Then the baby got down to business and got it over with efficiently. His delivery was picture-perfect. I was able to watch him emerge in the mirror Dr. Lechner again provided.

John was a beautiful, blonde, blue-eyed, dimpled baby. Even his knees had dimples! He loved to be held and petted; I had a baby to cuddle once more. In just a few short weeks, he was cooing and gurgling joyfully at every face looming over his basket. He was the epitome of the cuddly infant in sentimental paintings.

He had a shopping cart full of faces smiling at him, and he soon smiled back. There were Gail's and David's multiple times a day; mine, of course — frequently; Bill's in the morning and evening — several times an evening; Bill's mom's many times a week; my father's regularly — a quick detour to say hello to the children and admire his namesake in the morning and then again on his way home from work.

My good friend, Mary, who lived just down the block, was the "Earth Mother" type who stopped in frequently with her two children. They played with Gail and David while Mary and I enjoyed a cup of tea — and admired Johnny. Mary loved to pick him up, cuddle him, bounce him on her knee, make him laugh. He had every reason to be the happy baby he was.

But then, when he was 11 months of age, Johnny developed an ear infection. He cried as if his heart would break. Nothing satisfied him. I took him to the doctor and he was given a course of antibiotics. I thanked Heaven for those new miracle treatments. If he had been born only a few short years earlier, I thought, that miracle drug would not have been available; I expected a cure in short order.

But it was a stubborn infection despite those antibiotics. We would believe it was over and done with, and Johnny's smiles would return for a few days. Then, suddenly, the smiles would disappear and he'd begin to scrub at his ear with his fist. We'd hurry back to the doctor for more antibiotics. Almost as soon as it seemed to be cleared up, it would be back.

That went on for months. John's sunny nature turned stormy. He became a fearful child. He began to identify every touch with pain, and cried heartbrokenly over the least fright or unexpected touch. If he awakened in the night, he'd sob and sob and need to be walked in our arms for what seemed hours. If he even touched his ear with his little pumping fist, he'd shriek in fear of pain and thrash around in our arms as if to escape.

We were frantic. The doctor could find no sign of more infection, there was no fever, but John was so wary of anything touching that ear that his smiles and happy chuckles disappeared from the face of the earth. He would lie quietly when he was awake, but he never seemed as contented as before — it seemed almost as if he were just waiting for the pain in his ear to attack again.

John no longer ate his food with gusto. He'd accept the spoon I put into his mouth and swallow, but there were no waving arms, no laughter. There seemed no sunlight in his life. He became a wary, wan baby, often startled into tears. My mother-in-law was wonderful with him. He responded to her with acceptance, but my father was devastated when his namesake cried upon seeing him enter the door. Mary, who cuddled and bounced and tickled Johnny before the ear infections, lifted him from his crib for a cuddling, but he threw himself back away from her. She tried to jolly him, but — sobbing and reaching for me — he'd have none of it.

If John disturbed in the night, he awoke shrieking in fear. Bill, or I, or often both of us, bolted out of bed to his crib. When we picked him up, he thrashed around in our arms, almost out of control. We took him to the E.R, to the doctor, but nobody could understand why he was reacting so violently.

It was months before Johnny began to calm down somewhat. He was never again the happy, cuddly *baby* he had been. But, once he finally outgrew those serial ear infections, he did become a happy *child.*

By the time he was a pre-schooler, his delightfully infectious laugh once again encouraged laughter around him. The teachers at nursery school — when another child cried — would find something to make Johnny laugh. The sound was so compelling that soon all the children were again in good moods. One of the teachers dubbed him "the smile-maker."

John developed empathy early. If another child cried, John's face clouded. His face grew long when he saw others hurting. A few years later, when his youngest sister Anne, still an infant, suffered a fall, Bill and I rushed her off to the hospital, leaving 14-year-old Gail in charge of John and Beth. John, perhaps as a result of all that pain with his ear infections, or possibly genetically programmed for it, took after his Grandfather Keeber as a champion worrier. Compulsively concerned about Anne, he pestered Gail with incessant questions about whether his baby sister would die. Since Gail was with Anne when the baby fell, she was a basket case already, even though she was not responsible for the accident. David came to Gail's rescue, sternly ordering 10-year-old John to "Go find something *useful* to do!"

Bill and I returned home with the baby — only frightened, not really damaged. Gail, David and Beth clustered around her joyfully. But John was missing. We found him on his knees in his bedroom intently praying aloud for his baby sister to be all right. At David's command, he found "something useful to do."

As a grown man, John is still a caregiver. He hovered over his grandmother when she was old and ailing, suffering with her over whatever bothered her. He is a sympathetic and caring adult.

But baby John, barely starting to walk, had nowhere near conquered his fears and incessant tears when I realized my period was late again. It was too soon! I had my hands full with John and David and Gail. How could I possibly be pregnant again? We had been ever so careful. How could this *be*?

I *was* pregnant, without a doubt. There would only be 15 months between John and the new one. Then, perhaps two months into the pregnancy, I developed sciatica. I could barely move. I couldn't pick up Johnny at all, nor bend to David and Gail. In agony, I was ordered by Dr. Lechner to lie flat on the couch to rest the nerves involved till they stopped jangling. Gail, still a pre-schooler, automatically tried to assume responsibility for her two brothers. But Mom K's help was urgently needed.

I remember thinking, as I lay there, "Is a big family really such a good idea?" I wasn't prepared to "give back" any one of the children, but I couldn't help wondering how we could possibly manage with me incapacitated.

There was no lovemaking then. I was afraid to even turn over in bed. Bill was solicitous, taking over more and more of the care of the children and more and more of the daily housework when he was home. But, between school and work, he wasn't home a lot of the time.

For the first couple of days, Mom Keeber came to the house daily to help. She lived only blocks away. Then, as it became obvious I could do almost nothing, she simply moved in, once more sleeping on the couch at night after I vacated it. She did our marketing, cooking, laundry; she changed Johnny. We could not possibly have survived that problem without her help.

Eventually, after several weeks, the sciatic pain subsided but at first, I was fearfully careful how I moved to avoid any possibility of recurrence. But the pregnancy proceeded in the same healthy way my others (except for that temporary worry with David's) had done. The doctor said the developing baby had moved higher in my belly and was no longer resting on my sciatic nerve. I began looking forward to the delivery, wondering if we'd have a boy or a girl. I was still careful of my back, but I could again care for the children and do housework. Mom K no longer had to sleep on our couch.

Things, however, were more difficult for me than in earlier pregnancies since John was so young and easily upset and Gail and David were more and more active. They kept me so busy! With their adventurous exploits, I had to visit the E.R. with one or the other about once a week.

Late in my fourth pregnancy, when the intake nurse saw me waddling in carrying a limp child, she looked up brightly to ask, "Which one is it this time, Mrs. Keeber?" I was shocked! To be known by name at the E.R. was not the sort of fame to which I aspired!

Bill was plugging away at his studies, working as many hours as he could to supplement his student stipend. I was chugging along trying to keep my head above water with an old house to keep, three-and-a-half children — three very active at my feet and the "half" beginning to feel equally active in the womb. Life seemed a steady round of work, work, work, sleep a little, wake for a crying baby, snatch a quick doze, wake for breakfast, laundry, cooking, cleaning, fall asleep, wake in the night to Johnny's cries, wake in the mornings to demands for more food, laundry, cooking, cleaning. It was a never-ending treadmill.

I questioned again the wisdom of wanting a large family. But I tried to tell myself this was just a phase. It would all improve soon. I knew it would. It had to. And it did … in time.

THE GRIM REAPER - AGAIN

David was still an infant when my grandmother's health failed. She had been such a rock throughout my life! Taking over my care whenever Mother was laid low with her disabling headaches, Grandma schooled me in her strong ethic of courage, reliability, practicality and manners. She inspired me with stories of her heroic life and taught me to be ready for the love of a good man with her fond tales of her own two loves.

When Grandma died, I felt as if the floor had fallen away beneath my feet, but I barely had time to mourn; I was so busy with two small children. Despite the ache in my heart, I tried not to let the children see my sadness. Nor did I want to pain Mother with my grief, since hers was such a heavy burden to her. Grandma had supported and helped her all her life and, although Mum was then working in the office rather than straining her physical ability at home, the loss was far worse for Mother than for me.

While I had not been close to Mum in my earlier years, I came more and more, as an understanding adult, to admire her courage under fire from her continually-stressed health. We spoke by telephone or in person almost daily. She loved to hear of the children's doings. Then, when John was just three weeks old, two days after she so enjoyed his Christening Day, Mother suffered a massive stroke and was gone in an instant.

I had a wakeful night, knowing something was wrong. I tiptoed to look in on the children. I checked doors and windows, then went back to bed, still uneasy. When the phone rang that morning at 7:30, I leaped out of bed and caught it before the second ring. My father's voice said, "Bea? You'd better sit down. I have a bad shock for you." "It's Mother, isn't it?" I asked him immediately. I knew without another word that she was gone. I don't know how I knew; there was no warning, no health crisis out of the ordinary, but I knew.

At the funeral home, gathering my composure in the ladies' lounge after a tearful meeting with Mother's office friends, I felt uneasy about deserting Dad's side for those moments; he was so dazed and unbelieving. Then, as if hearing Mother's voice in my ears, words sounded in my head. "There's no need to cry. You can be strong! I'm well now and happy, but worried about you and your dad. Be a help to Dad."

I was comforted, my heart soothed, more at peace with Mother's passing. I was able to contain my own sadness and take over most of the activity of those visitation hours and the funeral, shielding Dad from as much pain as I could. He later thanked me for being a "tower of strength" for him and told me he didn't think he could have survived those days without me at his side. I knew I could not have supported him so firmly without those comforting words in my head and my heart.

Dad was a train-wreck. He and Mother had spent every moment together. Together to and from the office and there all day, they prepared dinner and spent evenings together, too. As a 25th anniversary gift to themselves five years earlier, they enjoyed a wonderful month-long cross-country vacation. They were planning more travel in their upcoming retirement. Travel brochures and AAA Travel Guides were often spread out on the dining room table for them to study together.

With the loss of his love and constant companion, Dad was again overwhelmed by the emotions of being orphaned as a child, but even more devastatingly, since he then had his supportive older brother and loving older sister to care for him and his two young sisters; he had his family in his daily life. With Mother gone, the mother-in-law he had loved as if she were his own mother gone, too, and me married, he was totally alone in the echoing house. It was impossible for him to sleep in their bedroom. He sat up nights in the living room, setting afire first one, then another chair, then the couch as he fell asleep with cigarettes in his hand. Each time, he awakened in time to drag them, smoldering, out the front door. I feared for his life! Every other day, I bundled up the children to drive to Dad's house where I found ashtrays overflowing and two days' worth of dishes pushed back on the table. If I waited another day, they might have fallen off the other end as he absently pushed them back after the breakfasts he made for himself (something he had done all the years of his marriage), and the meals I cooked and left for him to re-heat. He routinely scorched those in the warming. Crusty pots and dried-on plates awaited me each time I arrived at the house with the children.

I scoured pots, scrubbed plates, cleaned the stove, sink, table, did Dad's laundry, put the house in order, left him one meal ready in a low oven, another in the refrigerator before dashing home in the late afternoons to make dinner for Bill and the children. Totally lost in his own empty house — no longer a home — Dad was miserable alone. Stopping at our house did little to help him. He was painfully assaulted with memories of Mother there, too, enjoying the children on their frequent stops en route home from work.

Dad grew thinner and pale, more and more wan. Alarmed, my Aunt Elsie, Mother's dearest sister, invited him to stop at her house for dinner every couple of nights, then asked some of her widow friends to dinner those same nights. Dad desperately needed company to help draw him out of his abysmal grief and those widows understood what he was experiencing. Soon, one of the ladies began to invite Dad to meals at her own house, plied him with dinners, cakes, cookies, companionship and care.

Within a year, Dad was remarried and happily embarked on tandem living again. I was grateful to see him smiling once more, regaining the weight he had lost. His first marriage lasted 30 years, his second another 15. Mabel, my step-mother, and I were never close. She was possessive over Dad's time. He often visited me and the children as part of this errand or that, rather than try to convince Mabel to make the trip with him. Nevertheless, I was glad to see Dad happy again. He was not suited to living alone.

GROCERY EXPEDITIONS

After Bill's early help when we were first married, I got the hang of marketing pretty quickly. But with children, it became progressively more strenuous. Without a car, I traveled to the supermarket and brought groceries home under foot power.

With only Gail, it wasn't difficult; I just placed grocery bags beside her feet in the carriage. When David arrived, Bill built a "jump-seat" for the carriage, to fit across the foot of the conveyance. Gail could sit on that with David inside. Then Bill rigged a method of draping across the carriage several ropes with hooks on each end. I sewed up sturdy cloth bags with handles to hold the groceries, and hung them on the hooks in a non-elastic bungee-cord effect. Traveling home, David's body was hidden by the ropes, with just enough space left for Gail's knees to fit between them and her seat. Dangling bags decorated both sides of the carriage. With a brighter paint job on it and a few bells, we might have passed for a traveling gypsy wagon!

On one such shopping trip with Gail and David, I was approached by an impeccably-suited lady with little dead foxes in a fashionable circlet around her neck. She wore a fox fur hat atop her perfect silver hairdo. Peeking into the carriage at David in his blue outfit, she asked coyly, "A little boy?" "Yes," I told her. "Isn't he adorable?" she exclaimed. Then turning to Gail, she enthused, "And what a darling little girl! One of each — oh my! You are so fortunate! How far apart are they in age?" "Twenty-two months," I responded, beaming proudly.

"Well, my dear," she said, looking me sternly in the eye, her smile suddenly a thing of the past. "Now you have a girl and a boy. That must surely be enough! You know, this doesn't have to go on." Shocked, I caught my breath. She reached into her bag for a brochure about birth control and tried to hand it to me.

When, before marriage, Bill and I agreed we wanted a big family, we reasoned that our children — with no uncles, aunts or cousins — would have too few relatives for a solid support system unless we ourselves provided them. Over the years, our plan proved successful. Our five adult children stay in frequent touch with one another cross-country and meet whenever possible. Even the far-flung next generation of eight cousins stays in contact via Facebook. We two "onlies" *did* succeed in building the supportive, caring family we envisioned.

I pushed away the woman's brochure, saying, "No, thank you, I'm not interested." "But, my dear," the woman persisted, "You really don't have to continue having babies! Please *do* read this," she begged.

I shoved away her hand. To discourage her, I said, "None of that will work; my husband refuses to wear pajamas to bed." For good measure, with a flip of my hair, a shrug of my shoulder, and a wicked grin, I added, "And I don't *want* him to, *either!*"

Horrified at the unspeakable concept of multiple births as a result of wanton sexuality rather than feminine submissiveness, she caught her breath, pocketed her brochures and fled! Thoroughly invigorated, I finished the marketing and cheerfully pushed the grocery-laden carriage home.

When I told Bill of the encounter, always oriented to the details, he was mystified. "But I do wear pajamas to bed." "Honey, you're missing the point," I said. "I drove off that nosey busy-body!" He smiled and nodded, but I think my satisfaction over the event remained a mystery to him.

On another expedition with Gail and David, I made it up the hill to the last of the three markets between which I comparison-shopped. I started to choose those items on my list which were most reasonable at that market. Although Gail was usually helpful, it was a crabby day for her. After the long climb pushing the carriage uphill, I was running short of nice myself.

Gail was dressed, as was customary at the time, in a carefully ironed dress and fluffy petticoat, with a ruffled diaper cover over that necessity. With her bright blue eyes and bobbing strawberry blond curls, she was as cute as a button. She reluctantly trailed me through the aisles, touching things, begging for items not on my list. When she unintentionally knocked down an artfully arranged tower of canned goods, "cute" ran out and my patience reached its limit.

I repaired the display, then with one knee on the floor, bent Gail over my other one and spanked her. The action was cautionary rather than vengeful. Through the copious ruffles and the bulky diaper itself, I doubt Gail felt much at all. But she loudly roared her displeasure at the indignity.

A well-intentioned shopper bustled up to berate me for spanking my toddler. Reflexively, I picked up Gail and shoved her at the woman, who automatically put up her hands to "catch" the baby. I snarled, "If you think you can do a better job, *go right ahead!*" then turned my back and rapidly walked away.

Gail's blood-curdling shriek caused instantaneous reaction. The woman chased me down the aisle to apologize for "interfering" and to rid herself of hysterical Gail as quickly as she could. I grimly grabbed the child, Gail's screams ceasing on the instant. Plunking her down on her feet, I turned and marched on down the aisle with Gail behind me, silently gripping my skirt hem in her fist. Some shoppers glared at me, others clapped as the other woman retreated.

When John came along, a different marketing procedure had to be devised. I settled Johnny into the carriage, tucked a coil of rope under the foot of his mattress, and placed David on the wooden seat. That arrangement required continually monitoring the position of David's feet to be sure he wasn't indulging in furtive sibling rivalry. (I think it's a boy thing; Gail never tried to kick David when she occupied that seat!) I pushed the carriage. Gail walked beside it, pulling Bill's old American Flyer express wagon fitted with its slatted sides. It was about five blocks to the nearest of the three supermarkets.

Arriving at the first market, I parked John, sleeping in the carriage, at the front in view of the cashiers. With David in the grocery cart and Gail alongside, I walked the aisles, jotting down the price of each item on my list. Then we moved on with our carriage-wagon-train to the second grocery store half a mile away. I again placed carriage, John and wagon in view of the cashiers and repeated my price recording.

After another half mile uphill to the third market, I purchased whatever was least expensive there. With bags of groceries hanging off the carriage and fitted into the wagon, we set off downhill. I maneuvered the carriage with one hand, bending over to restrain the back of the wagon with the other one so it wouldn't overtake Gail's heels as she steered it downhill. At the second shop, I purchased all the most-reasonably-priced items there, then completed my marketing with the final bargains at the first one.

By the time we were ready to head home, the wagon — no longer trundling downhill — was too heavy for Gail to pull and, besides, she was tired of walking. I was careful to pack into bags at the front of the wagon the non-crushable items capable of bearing weight. Gail rode atop those, happy to sightsee from the enhanced height. With the wagon roped to the carriage's handlebar at a convenient length for me to reach behind for the wagon's grip to steer it with one hand, I push-pulled the combination those last five blocks home.

Arriving there with hungry, tired children, I drag-bumped the wagon up two steps into the shed behind the kitchen for safety from neighborhood dogs. Unloading only the perishable goods to stow them quickly in the refrigerator, I fed the children and put them down for naps. Then I had time to unload the remainder of the purchases and put those away. That done, I treated myself to a cup of tea and a short "sit-down" before I managed to dredge up enough energy to make my own lunch — if I didn't doze in the chair instead.

Shortly before Beth was born, Bill and I finally became the pleased owners of a used car. The purpose of the purchase was to shorten Bill's commuting time between school, work and home, but he took the bus on marketing days. Horsepower rather than mother-power made shopping easier, but it still wasn't a stroll in the park. After Beth's arrival, although my weight hovered just above or just below only 100 pounds, I had to fold the carriage and lift it both into and out of the trunk a total of six times. The baby had to be transferred into or out of the infant car carrier each time we made another stop. But still it was better than that long walk, especially the trip home pushing the carriage and dragging the express wagon, both heavy with groceries and tired children.

NEIGHBORS

City homes come complete with neighbors. They live in close proximity where houses are only as far apart as the width of the sidewalks leading to their back doors. Unless you are deaf and blind, you *will* become acquainted with neighbors based on their nearness. Ours were an education to me.

I had lived in the suburbs, where my friends' parents had similar values, habits, and looked like us. My mother was one of five siblings. My aunts, uncles and cousins were much like Mother, Dad, Grandma and me in their customs, beliefs and general behavior. By the time Bill and I bought our house in Cold Spring, the neighborhood was rapidly evolving into a spicy stew of residents from varied backgrounds. I had no prior experience with diverse populations.

Fortunately, my parents, Scottish and English immigrants themselves, schooled me in what they termed "democratic principles." Although unacquainted with the mores, habits and peculiarities of nationalities, cultures, races different from my own, I was at least well prepared to accept them. That background stood me in good stead in Cold Spring as we met our new neighbors.

THE CONNAUGHYS

The family next door to our new house, the Connaughys, came from Ireland. They spoke with a lovely, musical lilt in their voices. I rarely saw Mr. Connaughy since he worked long hours, but it was obvious Mrs. Connaughy did. They had several tall, strapping, dark-haired, square-jawed, blue-eyed, extremely handsome sons. I never figured out the exact number, since there was such a family resemblance between them all.

Mrs. Connaughy shared housekeeping advice with me, leaning her sturdy arms on the fence as I hung laundry or supervised the children's play in our postage-stamp-sized back yard. She was a short, solid-looking woman who was well able to keep a number of active sons in line. She had fair skin, freckles, friendly azure eyes (which flashed blue fire whenever she had to discipline her boys) and wavy, sandy-grey hair pulled back into a loose knot. Her sons were eager to be helpful. If they saw me dragging a garbage can to the street, they'd raise the container to their shoulders and carry it to the curb. If I actually reached the street with it myself, they smilingly berated me for not asking them to do it.

There was busy bicycle traffic in and out of their yard, loud bike races in the street. Sometimes the boys played ball or roughhoused together in their back yard … with a lot of yelling and action and laughter. I was called upon to lob the ball back over the fence if it came my way while I hung out laundry. Then they would laughingly engage me for a few more throws.

One unforgettable time, I really appreciated those cheerful boys' help. I called out my kitchen window to tell them my problem. Cities are often plagued by rats and our old neighborhood had its fair share. Our current cat enthusiastically cleaned out a whole family of baby rats, proudly depositing them on the side porch at the kitchen door, on the doorstep from the shed to the garden, and on the front doorsill and stairs. There was no exit not decorated with dead rats. Repelled, I called out my kitchen window for help from those strapping boys. Two of them dashed over with a shovel and a sack to clean up the cat's leavings, while a couple more filled buckets from our backyard hose to slosh away all evidence of the massacre.

The Connaughys were a happy, noisy, helpful family. It was fun living next door to them!

MRS. HURECK AND HAL

Mrs. Hureck, the lady living in the house on the other side, was originally from a rural village east of the city. She told me she was one of "a great, big, Polish farm family." Widowed young during the Great Depression, she came to Buffalo with her late husband's life insurance settlement and their three small children — seeking employment to enable her to raise them. Mrs. Hureck, when I knew her, was a short, stout, pink-cheeked, energetic lady with iron-gray hair pulled back into a taut no-nonsense bun. A few curly wisps always escaped the rubber band and bobby pins. She was usually smiling and cheerful with sparkling, intense brown eyes.

Finding no job awaiting her when she first arrived in the city, she rented the three-bedroom house next door, and finished the attic herself to make a fourth bedroom she shared with her children. She divided that room into male and female halves with a homemade curtain down the center. She furnished the living room as a bedroom, separated it from the dining room with another curtain, turned the dining room into a sitting room, and placed in the roomy kitchen a large dining table. Then she took in roomers, two to a bedroom, eight in total. She charged extra for meals and their personal laundry. That garnered enough cash, which — added to her small widow's Social Security check and her children's Social Security dependents' allowances — enabled her to raise her two sons and one daughter through the Depression years. But her income progressively decreased to less, less, and still less as her children reached their majorities and their Social Security Survivors' Benefits ceased. After her children grew up and moved away, Mrs. Hureck continued to receive her small monthly widow's Social Security check based on her deceased husband's employment during the short years of their marriage, but Mrs. Hureck then went out daily to clean other people's homes in the more prosperous areas of the city to enhance her income.

One of her roomers was Hal, a barber who worked in Cold Spring. Hal was pale, tall, slim, stooped, with thin silver hair and light blue eyes. Unless chatting in his quiet way, he was usually seen with a somber expression on his long face. He always reminded me of a sad-looking hound dog with a limply wagging tail.

As time went on, Mrs. Hureck and the barber developed a closer relationship. Mrs. Hureck eventually stopped working as a domestic and all the roomers but Hal moved out so she could "retire." (I never did learn Hal's surname. Mrs. Hureck always referred to him as "Hal-my-roomer.") Hal retired from barbering to live on a very small monthly Social Security income based on his rather meager lifetime earnings. He began to spend a lot of time on the porch rocker. Despite being "retired," Mrs. Hureck was rarely seen sitting; she always appeared to be cheerfully busy, periodically calling out comments and pleasantries to Hal on the porch, to which he nodded and responded, "Mm-HMMMMM." Sometimes she shouted, "Can you hear me, Hal?" He'd reply, "Yup, I hear you fine."

Mrs. Hureck's income from her services — cooking, washing and housekeeping for her roomers and cleaning in wealthy homes — was "unrecorded." She never earned wages under the Social Security system to be eligible for income based on her own earnings. From her work as a domestic, Mrs. Hureck managed to save some amount, which would, she hoped, see her through her old age without want.

Over the unpainted old board fence between our back yards, Mrs. Hureck confided to me the problem she and Hal faced. She was no longer earning money as a domestic, nor for taking in multiple roomers. She did not quality for Social Security herself and she was guarding her small cash nest egg for her later years. If she and Hal married, as they wanted to do, she would lose her widow's Social Security income. Two could not survive on Hal's small Social Security check. They could not afford to marry — so they just "lived together."

That would not be shocking in this day and age, but it was considered scandalous in the 1950s, so they continued the fantasy that Hal was Mrs. Hureck's roomer. That was a new concept to me. I had never met unmarried people who lived together as if married. I had never considered the sort of problem my neighbors faced. I sympathized with their economic strictures.

MRS. WHITE AND "UNCLE"

Across the street lived another couple of retirement age. They were very dark-skinned blacks. The husband was quiet, and alternated between rocking on the front porch and busying himself about the house and garden. He was of middling height, "substantial" but not overweight, with a warm smile. He was always pleasant and willing to stop his puttering to chat in his very soft-spoken way.

His wife was an ample, well-corseted lady who always wore white uniforms, white stockings and white shoes. In open-window weather, I often heard her vacuum cleaner. She also busied herself scrubbing their porch, the door, polishing the already-sparkling windows. Every summer evening, after dinner, she donned a totally fresh uniform, stockings and freshly polished shoes. Then she and her husband occupied a pair of rocking chairs on their immaculate front porch, with a small radio providing a soft background of Caribbean music as they chatted with passersby till dark fell. Between them, they kept their home and garden, as well as themselves, as tidy as a freshly painted picket fence.

When David was born, the wife came to our door with a huge bowl of fresh fruit, as she also did when John and Beth arrived. She urged me to eat plenty of fruit to regain my strength after the baby's birth. She frequently offered to babysit but I rarely accepted her offers except for unplanned trips to the doctor's office or the emergency room with one or the other of the children. I had no money to spend on myself, and couldn't then imagine what I would do with time on my own. Anyway, I was busy from wake-up to fall-asleep with my family.

My neighbor often walked across the street when the children were playing on the porch with the baby gate at the top of the stairs. She sat on the top step on the other side of the gate to play Peek-a-boo with them. I often invited her to open the gate, come in and have a glass of iced tea with me. But she always refused, saying she was fine where she was — she was happy just enjoying the children.

Because of her habitual white garb, Gail called her Mrs. White. She seemed to like that. I occasionally asked her correct name, but she would chuckle melodiously and tell me, "'Mrs. White' is just fine." She often pointed out to the children her husband sitting on their porch. "Wave to him!" she told them, "Say 'Hello, Uncle!'" He always smiled and waved back. She frequently brought freshly baked goodies across the street to me, saying I was too thin, and needed "a few more bites" to put some meat on my bones.

I confessed to Bill that I was a little uncomfortable calling her "Mrs. White" since that was only the name Gail bestowed upon her. I told him, friendly as she was, she seemed reluctant to tell me her real name. But, over time, I did become accustomed to addressing her as "Mrs. White."

MR. AND MRS. FISHER

About halfway down the block on our side, there lived a gentle, sweet-faced, elderly, light-skinned black lady, Mrs. Fisher. She and her husband, with none of their own, raised a huge number of foster children. She was tiny and thin, bright-eyed and full of energy. Her husband's skin was more grayish than tan. He was also small but as bent as a parenthesis, and he moved slowly. In their old age, with no more children to care for, she polished the interior of her house and the windows, swept the porch and sidewalk frequently. Mr. Fisher still went out to work daily with his lunch pail, leaving very early in the morning, returning home just before dinnertime. I never knew where he worked.

As time went on, Mrs. Fisher's mind began to wander. She was still bright and cheerful, but often confused. Sitting on her front porch when a neighbor said hello to her, she asked hopefully, in her reedy, high voice, "Are you one of my children come back to see me?"

She left her house less and less. Leaves accumulated on their porch, windows no longer shone. Her husband still went to work daily. He looked as old as the hills. His wife's hair was snow-white and thin. She seemed almost birdlike with her spare, bony frame.

Early one summer morning, I stepped onto the front porch to take in our delivery of milk. I was surprised to see Mrs. Fisher limping along the sidewalk. Looking closely, I saw that she wore one high-heeled shoe and one fuzzy bedroom slipper. On her head was a straw hat with a bobbing flower. From beneath the hem of a dress at least two sizes too large for her, I could see the bottom edge of what was clearly a long flannelette nightgown. From each wrist dangled a handbag, one black, the other a brightly patterned red. She wore one green glove. "Good morning!" she said cheerfully, noticing me on my porch. Her nod of greeting agitated the flower on her hat into frantic motion. "Good morning," I replied hesitantly, still inventorying her outfit. "I've been invited out to breakfast! I have to hurry!" she told me gaily. "Oh, that's nice," I replied. In her eagerness to be on time for her appointment, she continued on down the street, waving one hand cautiously at me, careful not to dislodge the bright red handbag.

She tottered past our house and on to the corner. There, she crossed the street to the other side, turned and came back on the opposite sidewalk. She waved happily to me again as I continued to watch her. Crossing the street in mid-block to her own house, she limped briskly up the porch steps, rang the doorbell, then opened the door and stepped in!

I tried to watch for her husband when I thought he might be coming home. It seemed he ought to know about her adventure, but he must have passed when I was busy making dinner. I never had the chance to tell him.

KIDNAPPED!

When Gail was just a toddler, she caught people's attention with her bright blue eyes and bobbing strawberry-blonde curls, which appeared to catch fire when sunlight struck them. Gail was prepared to be friends with everyone. There were no strangers in her world; only more friends she had not yet met. I used to put an array of toys on the porch for Gail, place David's playpen out there with her, and fasten the safety gate at the top of the steps. I usually used the "free" time thus derived to iron in the living room. From there I could check on them frequently through the windows while safely plying the hot appliance without the children endangered underfoot.

One afternoon, before John was born and shortly after Mrs. Fisher's "breakfast date," I walked back to the kitchen to change the load of laundry, stopped to fold the dried towels, then returned to the front window to look out on the children. David played contentedly in his playpen, but I could not see Gail. I dashed out to the porch. The safety gate was still firmly latched. But Gail was gone!

I dashed across to Mrs. White, who ran back to my porch to oversee David while I started searching. "Uncle" walked up and down the sidewalk calling Gail's name. I checked our back yard, then ran to Mrs. Hureck's yard and searched there. I knocked on her door to tell her Gail was missing. She hurried to look in more back yards. I ran to the Connaughy's and rang their doorbell to ask for help. Mrs. Connaughy and the boys fanned out calling for Gail up and down the street. I alerted neighbors I barely knew and they immediately turned out and started searching, too.

After three quarters of an hour, with no sign anywhere of our toddler, I called the police. They joined the search, terrifying me as they lifted garbage can lids and shone flashlights into crawl spaces under porches and houses. Gail seemed to have vanished into thin air!

I called Mom K, who arrived in moments, breathless and overheated. She started searching, too. I called the university office and someone found Bill, who immediately caught a bus to come home. The entire neighborhood appeared to be involved. But there was no sign of Gail! Another hour-and-a-half dragged on. I was tearfully wracked with fear for her safety. Despite his own worry, Bill tried unsuccessfully to convince me she *must* be all right. Mrs. White took David home with her to rock him to sleep on her own porch.

Finally, Bill and I stood holding hands at the front steps, our hearts heavy, not knowing where else to look. Mom K sat on the bottom step silently shredding her handkerchief. A few neighbors drifted back into their homes to start making dinners. Uncle, Mrs. Hureck, Hal, and the Connaughys kept searching, as did the police.

Mr. Fisher came shuffling along the street on his way home. One of the Connaughy boys told him of Gail's disappearance. He stopped to tell us, "I'm so sorry to hear of your worry. I'll pray for her safe return."

Our hearts like lead, we thanked him for his consideration and his prayers. He continued to his own house, disappearing from our sight as he turned onto the walk to his back door.

Only seconds later, he burst out the front door, shouting, "I found her! I found her! She's safe! She's alright!" Bill, Mom and I dashed down the street. So did a policeman and several neighbors. We rushed into the Fishers' front room to see Gail on Mrs. Fisher's lap, a cookie in her hand and crumbs on her lips. Gail's clothes were neatly folded on the end table. She was wrapped in a large towel. Mrs. Fisher was brushing her sparkling coppery-wet curls, pulling out one curl at a time, then watching it spring back. She crooned tunelessly to Gail, whose eyes were heavy.

Gail seemed entirely content, concentrating on her cookie, until she saw me and reached out. I snatched her up, startling Mrs. Fisher, who said, "But I need to dry her before she catches cold! She just had a bath and her hair is still wet!"

Mr. Fisher was standing between his wife and the scowling police officer, telling him, "She didn't mean anything! She don't know what she's doing! Don't be mad at her — she don't know what she's doing! She was just trying to look after her!" It took quite a while to sort it all out. Mrs. Fisher must have come down the street, noticed Gail on our porch, assumed she was one of her long-gone foster babies. She reached over the gate, picked her up and took her home where she thought she belonged. Gail would have been quite happy to adventure off with a new friend.

Nobody thought about Mrs. Fisher during the search because by then she was so rarely seen outdoors that no one imagined she would know anything about a missing neighborhood youngster. Her frantic husband's words did little to mitigate the police officer's frown. He had been joined by two other patrolmen, equally stern. Despite Mr. Fisher's efforts to stay between them, the scowling officers surrounded Mrs. Fisher. She began to look frightened. Her husband desperately tried to squeeze between the policemen.

Bill stepped in and said to the senior officer, "Sir, I think I know what happened. This lady raised many, many foster children. Her mind is wandering in her old age. She thought Gail was one of her charges. I'm sure she believed she was taking her back home to look after her. She meant no harm." Mr. Fisher's eyes filled with tears. He added, "No Sir, she didn't mean no harm a-tall! She didn't know folks was lookin' for this child!" Several of the neighbors then crowding the room added, "She didn't mean any harm to the child." "She just wanted a baby to care for!"

Nowadays, social workers would be called in. Everyone there would be interviewed on record. An investigation would occur. Mrs. Fisher might be taken into custody and remanded to the county old folks home, the asylum for the insane, or even jail to await the outcome of the inquiry over several weeks' or months' time. But back then, things were worked out in a much simpler way. The senior policeman asked Mr. Fisher where he worked and if he needed the income. He was told Mr. Fisher continued to work "just to keep busy." It was soon settled that the police would make no charges if Mr. Fisher would just stay home from then on to take care of his wife. He agreed readily, eager to prevent any harm or blame coming to her.

We gathered up Gail's clothes. By then, her head was on my shoulder; she was asleep. Bill again told the police we had no intention of pressing charges. We told Mr. Fisher we were sorry for his trouble. He stuttered that he was sorry for *our* trouble. We took our little girl home, awakened her to try to feed her, but she wasn't hungry, filled with Mrs. Fisher's cookies. Mrs. White knocked on the door and brought David home with his emptied bottle.

The children were put to bed and were soundly sleeping. Bill, my mother-in-law and Mrs. White, who insisted on settling David into his crib herself, sat quietly on the front porch for a few minutes. Mrs. White stirred, then said, "You did the right thing. Her husband will look after her all the time now. She needs that." My mother-in-law nodded. She looked tired and drawn. The fright had taken a toll on her. She said she'd be going back home since we didn't need anything more. Mrs. White stood up, too. I hugged each of them. Bill thanked them both, then he went up and down the block ringing doorbells to thank all the neighbors who helped in the search.

Mr. Fisher came to the house the next day to thank us for not pressing charges against his wife. He said he didn't realize she was "that bad." He told me he'd take good care of her to see it could never happen again. Tears came to his eyes when he added that she might have been put in "the asylum" or "the home," and that it would just kill her to be among strangers. He soon left to return to her.

I was glad the officers had not acted too sternly in the wake of the kidnapping.

Hubby and Wife

Clear in my recollections of our interesting neighbors is another couple we never met face to face, nor did we ever learn their name. But we certainly never forgot them.

They lived a little more than halfway down the block on the opposite side of the street. They had several red-haired, stair-step sons who always played in their own tiny, fenced front yard. I never saw any other children playing with them. We rarely saw the wife outdoors, except when she emerged to settle a dispute between her boys. A small, wiry, dark-haired woman with snapping, brown eyes, she kept entirely to herself. Her husband was short and barrel-shaped, with a ruddy complexion, mild blue eyes and sandy hair.

In summertime, with our bedroom windows open onto the street, we would often hear the husband loudly singing his way home after the neighborhood bar closed. One night, shortly after our sleep was disturbed by Hubby musically wending his way home, we were wrenched totally from our bed by a loud commotion out on the street.

There were baritone yelps and imprecations screamed in a high soprano. Bill ran to one of the windows, I to the other.

There was Hubby racing down the middle of the street with not a stitch of clothing on him, his wife close behind him, barefoot, but running amazingly fast, her long, dark hair streaming out behind her. In one hand, she clutched the skirt of her nightgown hiked up to her waist. Her other hand wielded a butcher knife. Whoosh! It nearly reached her husband's buttocks. He speeded up.

She screeched at him that she'd had enough of this and intended to see that he never, *ever* had reason to wake her at such an ungodly hour of the night again. Whoosh! "Hubby" attained still more speed. Between swipes, the wife repeatedly yelled at him to stop and face her like a man — but he didn't appear at *all* well disposed to *that* idea! He gained greater speed each time the passing knife fanned his backside. The knife kept flashing, the wife kept screeching, the husband kept yelling for help. They continued down the middle of the street, rounded the corner and disappeared. Their voices faded into the distance.

We waited at the windows for a while. I said quietly to Bill, "Do you think they're coming back?" "I sure wouldn't if I were in his shoes — feet, I mean!" he replied. We looked at each other in the dim glow of the streetlight, shook our heads, and headed back to bed. As we settled in, my head on Bill's shoulder, his arms wrapped around me, he chuckled and muttered, "I think maybe I should take the knife sharpener to school with me tomorrow in case you get any ideas!" I giggled in the dark, cuddled closer, and we went back to sleep.

We never knew where they went after they rounded the corner nor what time they returned home. We never saw the wife unless she stepped out to referee a battle between her sons. When we moved away, they were still living in the house down the block, "Hubby" going to and coming from work each day. But we never again heard him singing his way home from the bar at night.

MOSES

Then there was Moses. He appeared on the scene our last summer in Cold Spring. He was a big boy for his age, which was probably close to Gail's. She was to start kindergarten that fall. Moses said he would be going to school then, too. His bare chest gleamed like mahogany in the sunlight, and he was proud to illustrate that he had biceps "jus' like the big boys." His family had recently moved into a house at the far end of the block. There seemed to be a lot of coming and going to and from the place, so I assumed they were sharing it with another family.

Moses asked me courteously if he could play with Gail, David and John, the current occupant of the playpen. I told him he could come in to play if he promised to tell me before he left so I could make sure the gate was safely latched again. He agreed, I opened the gate, he stepped up onto the porch and noticed that John had just tossed a rattle out of the playpen. It was a hiatus between earaches for John so when Moses picked it up and smilingly handed it back to the baby, John laughed delightedly. Without John noticing, Moses sneaked another toy out through the bars of the playpen to hand it to the baby. When John laughed again and reached for that toy, Moses grinned with satisfaction.

I returned to the living room, leaving the children to play by themselves while I wrote checks to pay bills. I could hear their every word. At first, it was mostly, "What's this?" from Moses, asking about the children's toys.

Gail was a "belle" from the day she was born. She charmed playmates and adults without even trying. When she became bored at Moses' fascination with her familiar toys, Gail commented to her new friend, "Moses, I'll bet you aren't strong enough to pick up my play table." Moses assured her he could pick up "anything." "Even my play table?" Gail asked. "Sure!" he responded, "Where's it at?" Gail led him into the house, past me in the living room, into her bedroom just off the dining room. Moses emerged, easily carrying Gail's play table. He marched to the porch, put it down with a thud, turned to her and said, "See? I tole ja I could!"

"You're right!" admired Gail, " ... But I'll bet you can't pick up both benches at the same time and carry *them* out here." "Sure I can!" he declared. "Show me!" Gail prodded. Moses marched determinedly back into the house with Gail right behind. He emerged from her bedroom with one bench under each arm, carried them past me, and plunked them down on the porch floor. "See?" he said for the second time. "I DO," agreed Gail, clapping her hands. "You *are* strong!"

Interested in whatever Gail suggested, Moses willingly played "tea party" with her and David. They each picked up a little tin flower-patterned cup and pretended to drink. Gail said, "Mmm-MMM, that's *good!*" just as she had often heard me exclaim with my first swallow of tea. David and Moses repeated her words. They played together for a little longer, then Moses decided he had to go home. Before he left, Gail somehow encouraged him to return her play table and the two benches to her bedroom. He told her he'd come back to play again, stuck his head in the door and asked me to open the gate. As I re-latched it, he sprinted rapidly toward home.

Moses returned several times that summer to play tea party with Gail and David. Each time, he carried Gail's play table and benches from the bedroom to the porch and returned them to her bedroom before he left. He unfailingly asked me to please open the gate before he left, as he promised the first time he came to play. He always found some toy on the floor to hand to Johnny with a smile, then slid another out of the playpen to hand him a second. Somebody had taught Moses excellent manners, but his cheerful disposition was his own.

Moses and Gail both started kindergarten that fall. One of the other mothers, seeing Gail talking to him, confided to me in a scandalized tone that Moses was "not good company" because his father had just gone to jail for selling drugs. ("Oh!" I thought, "*that's* why there was so much coming and going from that house!") But I told her that Moses had not sold drugs and since he was a well-mannered playmate, I saw no reason why Gail shouldn't play with him. Horrified, she yanked her little boy away from the two of them.

After school began, Moses did not appear as often to play. But when he did, Moses and Gail took turns on the swing in our back yard, then each took turns pushing David who couldn't yet "pump" it into motion. I could hear David's excited shrieks mingled with Gail's and Moses' laughter. I had moved the gate from the porch to the entrance to the back yard. Moses always remembered to knock on the kitchen door to ask me to open the gate so I could be sure it was latched after his departure. After the weather cooled, we didn't see Moses at all anymore except at the school.

BETHANIE LORRAINE

After an exhausting pregnancy, the start of school for Gail neared. I needed to take her and the other two to shop for her school shoes. It was close to the end of summer — hot and humid as only Buffalo-on-the-lake can be. I was too warm and too tired. The children were too warm and too tired. Somehow, despite rages and tears, we managed to find the necessary shoes and finally head for home.

It was still over a month before the new baby was due. But during dinner, I began to suffer what I hoped were cramps. They were not. That baby battled her way through labor as she battled her way through gestation — actively. Bill timed my contractions and when it seemed the right time, he called his mother to come care for the other children and drove me to the hospital.

There labor ceased for a while. Dr. Lechner, who prided himself on being there for both labor and delivery for his natural childbirth patients, relaxed in a chair enjoying a scholarly chat with Bill for a goodly part of the evening. Then he was called into a delivery. I dozed as he and Bill talked, and finally fell soundly asleep. Bill dropped off to sleep in his chair beside the bed.

In the early morning, the baby awakened me, suddenly in an eager hurry to join the family. "Bill!" I called out in alarm. "The baby's coming! I can feel the head!" Bill leaped out of the chair. Not yet fully awake, he ran blindly out the door — and smack into the opposite wall of the corridor. Reeling backward, he regained his equilibrium and disappeared down the hall, calling, "Dr. Lechner, Dr. Lechner!" Having observed his crash and recovery, I was howling with hysterical laughter in the labor room.

A very small nurse dashed into my room with a gurney, Bill right behind her. "Dr. L's still in another delivery!" panted Bill. I tried unsuccessfully to stifle my laughter. The nurse and Bill managed to move me, still giggling, from the bed to the gurney. Then the little nurse bravely attempted to slow the advance of labor to await the doctor's availability by holding my feet together. Of course, that hurt and the laughter ended abruptly. Without thought, motivated solely by the demands of my body at cross-purposes with the nurse, I yanked one foot out of her hand and kicked. The poor girl reeled backward across the room until she encountered the wall. She never complained — although later I would have agreed she had a right to — but she obviously wasn't sure what to do next.

"Bill, run this gurney down to Delivery! The baby's crowning!" I yelled. Bill raced me past the astonished nurse. Just as Bill, the gurney and I reached the doors of the delivery room, they opened. But before Bill could push my gurney in, another gurney emerged carrying the formerly-pregnant mother who delivered ahead of me. Dr. L ordered from inside, "No! Not this one — the next room!" He gestured toward the right. Bill turned and headed for another set of double doors. Just as he neared, the doors opened and he pushed the gurney inside. Dr. L was nowhere to be seen, but the room seemed full of large nurses. As one of them firmly pushed Bill back out the doors — no fathers allowed in delivery rooms! — another one moved my gurney to the center of the room.

"I want a mirror!" I wailed, noticing the lack. "No time for that, Missy!" said one officious lady. I could feel the baby moving into the world. Dr. Lechner emerged from the wash-up room trying to shake his hands dry, with a nurse energetically struggling to tie his fresh coat at the back of his neck. Another nurse held out gloves. He managed to wriggle into one. Just then, the baby shot out of my womb and into Dr. L's gloved hand there just in time to "catch" her, with the nurse still struggling to encase his other one. As soon as she succeeded, he lifted Beth for me to see, telling me, "You and Bill have another daughter!" She was tiny and red and howling like a banshee.

"Nothing wrong with this one!" he commented to the nurses. " — She has a lot to say about this indignity!" He placed her on my abdomen and she calmed as I stroked her head and then her body. He did what he had to do about the placenta, telling me to "push, push" as I expelled it. A nurse reached for Beth, but the delivery was so abrupt! My baby was so small! I was not yet ready to relinquish her. I resisted efforts to take her from me. I wanted to hold her and keep her safe. "Dr. L?" the nurse asked. "Let her stay here with her mommy for a while longer. She had a hard journey before she'd even packed," he told her calmly. The nurse stood back and waited.

After a moment or two more, I moved my hands away to allow her to lift Beth. She, too, may have been rattled by the unusually rapid delivery; she forgot to place a blanket on the scale. It must have been very cold. A howl like an injured wolf's erupted from that small body. Almost everyone in the delivery room froze at whatever they were doing, except Dr. L. He looked over at the nurse and said calmly, "Maybe you'd better bring her back here to Mother so she can warm up again." That time I wrapped my arms protectively around Beth, and she stopped wailing. The nurse said, rather shakily, "I think she's under five pounds, Doctor. She's probably a premie." I held Beth for what seemed a long time, but may only have been moments, until the doctor said, "The nurse has a nice warm blanket for her now."

The nurse draped a heated blanket over the baby and took her from my arms to weigh her again. Beth did clock in under five pounds. Although officially a premie, I heard her complaining fiercely in a full-sized voice as she was carried down the hall for Bill to see. When I was moved to the recovery room, Bill was allowed to see me. "She's so small!" he marveled. "She's all wrinkled and she's yelling blue murder!"

That was Beth's arrival on September 3rd, 1955, a month ahead of schedule. She arrived fighting and never stopped. She takes on life with fists doubled at the ready. Despite continuing to be miniscule all her life, she is as tough as nails. She rarely gives a quarter to events, but tries to shape them to her desires. Life has not been gentle with her, fighting back valiantly. Beth's pugilistic nature is finally slowing down a little in her late 50s, but she is still inclined to take on every challenge with vigor. After several bouts of chemo treatment, she appears to have won her battle over what had been described as chronic, incurable Hepatitis C. I'm convinced the virus was no match for that pint-sized dynamo, despite the fact that Beth gives credit to a new miracle drug and her doctors for the possibility of finally being declared "cured." Beth is loving, caring, tough, and able, and will probably never "give quarter" to the challenges life presents as long as she lives.

When I came home from the hospital with the new baby, the entire family was there waiting at the house, along with my friend Mary, who was to be the godmother. Mary made cooing sounds to the bundle in the blanket, but when the blanket was removed, Mom took one look and said frankly, "She hasn't an ounce of fat anywhere on her bones! She'd hardly made a decent chicken for the soup pot!" Mary gasped, but I had to laugh at Mom's accurate appraisal of our skinny little Amazon.

Over time, we decided that Bethanie Lorraine's name, lungs, and sense of adventure were all bigger than her entire body. She may have been tiny, but she had a strong will. She became a noisy, adventurous, innovative child who raced into each new experience at top speed — and *damn* the collateral damage! As a toddler, she was a frequent visitor to the E.R.

Beth tore through her infancy in mostly good health. Growing up, she rivaled her brother David for the distinction of being the most intrepid adventurer of the four siblings.

Beth is "one-of-a-kind." She meets life with her small bony fists at the ready and tries to mold it to her own will. She's not always successful, but I expect she'll keep trying 'til her last day. She is outgoing, chatty and friendly. Recently, we took her adult daughter to a bus station to return to her own home after the two visited me from opposite directions. While my granddaughter unloaded luggage, Beth rushed ahead to snag a spot in line for the traveler. Arriving inside the terminal, my granddaughter turned to me to say in wonder, "Look at her — she's amazing! In seconds, she has already made five friends and they're all talking to her at once." That's Beth.

HOW COULD WE POSSIBLY SPEND THAT MUCH MONEY?

Periodically, recruiters from a variety of businesses came to the university. Although committed to finishing his Ph.D. requirements, Bill enthusiastically attended those "job fairs" and filled out applications to begin to understand what opportunities awaited him in the workplace.

Bill successfully completed and presented his thesis for review, but still had to defend it. And he had one language requirement to complete, which he had put off several times; unlike me, he found languages a stumbling block. Bill's G.I. Bill entitlement ran out a year earlier, but he tested for and won a NY State veterans' scholarship. That, too, was due to expire at the end of the fall semester. Garnering money enough to continue through the end of the academic year was a major problem we had not yet solved. In the backs of our minds, we thought that a last resort might be for Bill to withdraw for a semester of full-time employment to earn and save enough money for his tuition and our survival for just that one final term.

In September, Bill was surprised to receive an offer from the company that eventually became Exxon-Mobil — for a position in their chemical research labs in New Jersey. He applied as a Ph.D., not really expecting to take a job till after his graduation. The monthly salary offered was so much more than we'd ever imagined possible! I asked Bill, "How could we possibly spend that much money in a month?"

Dazzled at the thought of a comfortable income after all those early years of scrimping, Bill took his offer to his tenured professor to ask his advice. His teacher, only a year short of retirement, told him "Grab it! That's more than I'm making NOW! Tell them you'll take your language requirement in the evenings somewhere in NJ and have the credit transferred. Offer to come back on your first vacation to defend your thesis. Don't miss this chance!" Bill decided tto follow his professor's suggestion. He conferred with the recruiter, who garnered approval for Bill to start work at the Ph.D. salary on the promise that he would complete the remaining course for his degree in NJ. Bill accepted the offer. We did find out how to spend that much money — New Jersey's cost of living was so much higher than Buffalo's! But it was still an amazingly generous offer, one Bill could not afford to reject.

Gail started kindergarten that Fall at Bill's old elementary school in Cold Spring. But times change. Even the walk to school for local children presented dangerous challenges Bill never knew – drunks, drug addicts, people with guns. With the area rapidly going downhill, we wished we could afford to move to a less-threatening neighborhood with the children, but — focused on Bill's tuition needs — we had not found a solution to that problem. The job offer and Bill's professor's advice provided the answer. Unexpectedly, with a good salary, the costs of Bill's remaining Ph.D. requirements and a better environment for the children were both within reach! Bill withdrew from the language class for which he had registered and requested additional hours at his part-time job. His employer was so pleased for Bill when he heard of his generous job offer that he gave him full-time work to tide us over until Bill left to start his new job.

We sold our house quickly for $5,500 — $2,600 more than we paid for it five years earlier! A nice-looking couple bought it, assuring us they loved it and couldn't wait to reside in it. We were pleased we could leave the little house we loved to good caretakers and happy for our neighbors to have nice new owners waiting to move in. Until then, our end of the block — encompassing our house, the Connaughy's, Mrs. Hureck's, and Uncle and Mrs. White's homes — was still a small haven from the encroaching blight on Waverley Street.

OLEY

In addition to a succession of cats, we had a parakeet. We named him Oley. I'm not sure why. The bird's cage hung in a corner of the dining room. When we opened his door, he zoomed around the living and dining rooms, relishing his freedom. He liked to settle on Bill's shoulder and nibble his ear, which always gave Bill shivers. He delighted the children by landing on their heads. Whenever he flew to my uplifted hand, I brought him close to my face, and he "kissed" me, touching my lips with his carefully closed beak. Then he tilted his head to look at me brightly, as if to say, "What a good boy am I!"

Oley's quirky sense of humor led to an unnerving new habit he developed. He zoomed through the rooms to gain speed, then folded his wings back and aimed himself directly for an adult's nose — turning into a turquoise projectile. (He didn't do it to children!) Most people dove for the floor in a panic. If an adult with steely nerves did *not* take a panicked dive, Oley daringly pulled up a mini-second before crash time, raking his victim's hair with his feet as he headed for the room's upper atmosphere. Then he landed on the top of his cage to chirp rapidly in a devilish mode that sounded remarkably like chuckling! We couldn't seem to break him of that habit; it became quite an annoyance.

One day, I crouched down to connect the vacuum hose. Oley must have launched himself from his cage door, aiming at my head. My back to the birdcage, I stood to activate the appliance. Crash! I saw stars! I grabbed my head in both hands, holding it tightly till the room stopped spinning. Then I saw Oley on the floor — on his back, his wings outspread. "Oh no!" I wailed. "He's dead!" As I tearfully reached for the bird, he flipped up one wing, turned over and landed on his feet, attained wobbly flight and settled himself in his cage. He just sat there with his head pulled down into his shoulders. He must have had a headache to rival the worst of hangovers! For two days, we didn't see him move even to eat or drink.

Finally, he walked carefully to the end of his perch to dip his head into the water container. He hunkered down again for a while, tried the water once more, then moved to his seed container and pecked at a seed. Gingerly cracking it in his beak … he appeared to decide he could stand the noise, so went back for more. Soon, he was joyfully launching himself from his cage doorway, zooming through the archway into the living room, circling the ceiling, then racing under the arch again before he headed back home for a drink and a snack. But Oley never dive-bombed anyone again.

Oley also imitated human sounds quite well. I cleared my throat frequently. Oley soon got that down pat and mimicked Johnny's laughter well, too.

Cold Spring then was far from the safe, familiar old neighborhood where Bill grew up. Shouts and gunshots were heard after dark and sometimes in daylight. At my friend Mary's house, a bullet crashed through a wall, crossed the kitchen only fractions of an inch above her daughter's head as she sat in her high chair eating lunch, and lodged in the opposite wall! The shooters were never identified. — When Bill left for NJ, I was nervous about staying there alone with four small children. Locking doors and windows and drawing blinds at early dusk to prevent intrusive eyes seeing in, I reassured myself that the Connaughys were right next door, and Mrs. Hureck and Hal would keep an eye on my house, too. So would Mrs. White and Uncle. …

Then, one night, there was a rape on the next block. The perpetrator was not caught. Groups of bold young men lounged on street corners, menacingly eyeing nervous passersby. The neighbors were very nervous.

By mid-October, I no longer allowed the children outdoors alone to play, even in our own little back yard; the swings hung unused. With all the children in tow, I walked Gail to and from P.S. Number Eight rather than allowing her to walk with a group of older grade-schoolers.

I stopped taking the children marketing with me. I took them to Mom K's and rushed through the shopping alone. Unless they were with Mom, I never allowed the children out of my sight; I was extra careful to keep doors locked even during the daytime.

On her last day at school, when I went to meet her, Gail told me that her teacher had all the children line up to give Gail hugs of farewell. She giggled when she told me about it, adding, "All the boys laughed when they had to hug me. But Moses laughed the hardest!"

When Bill flew home for Christmas, my dad picked him up at the airport and drove him home. It was so good to see him! We had never been apart before that, except for his two-day visit to New Jersey for his job interview or my hospitalizations when the children were born. It was so comforting to snuggle into bed with him, his arms wrapped around me again.

But much too soon, Bill had to leave again. After tearfully watching him drive away early on January 1st, my day with the children was particularly hectic. I was busy. Missing their dad, they were fussy and demanding. Beth required even more than her usual frequent feedings. I was exhausted by the time the children were settled in for the night. All I wanted was to fall into bed. But I was full of tired aches and pains and felt sure I would sleep more comfortably if I took time for a warm bath.

Over our years there, Bill and I occupied the front upstairs bedroom, installing the newest baby in the other upstairs bedroom. The older child or children used the bedroom off the dining room. But after Beth was born, before Bill left to start his new job, we moved the three older children to the two upstairs bedrooms and I lodged in the one downstairs with Beth. I felt more "on guard" on the ground floor.

With everyone settled in for the night, I dragged myself upstairs for a hot soak to ease away the soreness of the day. I threw my day's clothing into the hamper. When the comforting hot water cooled, I climbed out of the tub to dry. It was then I realized I forgot to bring upstairs my fresh pajamas. I had allowed myself only one towel to decrease the amount of last-second laundry. After drying myself and my hair, it was too wet to use as a wrap. There were no more in the bathroom; they were all packed. I would just have to make a run for it naked. After all, I was alone in the house except for the sleeping children. What difference would it make?

Opening the door of the steamy-warm bathroom, I was assaulted by winter's chill in the house. I ran as fast as I could down the stairs, heading for the dining room en route to the bedroom. Just as I tore through the dining room doorway, I heard a loud wolf-whistle at very close range! I skidded to a stop, my blood instant ice in my veins. Terrified, I thought of the unknown rapist. My throat closed. I couldn't scream for help; I couldn't even squeak. Then Oley did it again. It was Bill's "I'm home" whistle that Oley had never before tried!

I resumed my dash for the bedroom, fumbled into my warm flannelette pajamas and settled myself between the covers. Even though it was only Oley mimicking Bill's whistle, my body reacted; adrenalin took over, my heart pounded. Far from feeling sleepy and relaxed after my nice hot bath, I lay stiffly in bed, every muscle taut, nervously hearing the old house creak and groan as the wintry wind whipped around the eaves.

GOODBYE, HOUSE!

The day before we moved away, Mrs. White brought me a package of baked goods she made for us to take along on the airline, "in case the children need a snack." She added that I should be sure to make myself take time to eat more so I could gain a bit of weight. I missed Mrs. White and Uncle after we moved away. The children missed them, too. I'll bet Mrs. White and Uncle missed them as well.

I thought about Gail's friend Moses. I knew his father was in jail, and life must be very difficult for his mother. But someone taught Moses his good manners, and I assumed it must have been his mom. Moses was such a nice boy. In my heart, I wished him and his family well.

After leaving the baked goods with me, Mrs. White walked on down the street to tell Mr. Fisher we were moving away. He wanted to say goodbye to us so Mrs. White stayed with Mrs. Fisher while he came to see us. He wouldn't take time to come into the house, just stood on the porch at the front door to wish us well in our move. He told me he hoped we would be very happy in our new home. I wished him and Mrs. Fisher well, too. Watching him with tears in my eyes as he returned to his solitary care of his wife, I knew our future was so much more hopeful than his! ... Mrs. Connaughy came over to hug me and tell me she hoped Bill and I would have a wonderful life in N.J. The boys all came with her. Each one solemnly shook my hand and said, "Good luck, Mrs. Keeber!" ... Mrs. Hureck saw me outdoors and rushed out without a coat to give me a warm hug and tell me to have a good trip and a happy life. She called to Hal, who came outdoors shivering, solemnly shook my hand and said they'd miss us all.

It was finally January 4th! I awakened about 5:00 a.m., unable to sleep longer. The children were still quiet, so I dressed quickly, put on the kettle, and made myself a hot cup of tea. While I savored it, I looked up at the kitchen ceiling and thought of the work we so hastily put into it before we closed on our house purchase. I recalled the banker who took a chance on us with such an unusual mortgage arrangement. I remembered the multiple layers of wallpaper scraped off the walls before we could repaper them. I smiled as my eyes fell on the dishwasher, recalling the super-sudsing disaster. Looking toward the pantry doorway, I chuckled aloud, thinking of my mouse attack. I closed my eyes and tried to say goodbye to our well-loved first house.

I considered waking and dressing the children, but just then Beth began to fuss. Gail wandered sleepily downstairs as I finished feeding and diapering the baby. When I put her back into her basket, Gail reached in to gently stroke her cheek. We returned to the kitchen so I could make our breakfast. Hearing David coming down the stairs, I added another egg to the pan. The children were unusually quiet at breakfast that day.

Then Johnny started down the stairs. Gail hurried up the steps to take his hand. He was a very worried toddler. He was at the age where he didn't like change, and all the recent household activity upset him. I put out his favorite cereal, but he had little appetite. I knew today would be difficult for him. There would be more change in this one day than he had seen in his entire life. I sighed as he sucked his two middle fingers, wondering if his index and pinky fingers would poke dimples in his cheeks. They, or something, did. He hated those dimples when he was older!

My mother-in-law knocked and walked in. She was up bright and early to help us move. She saw John's fingers in his mouth and his full bowl of cereal. Lifting him onto her lap, she smilingly coaxed him to try bite after bite. This move would be hard on Mom. She loved our living nearby. She was widowed just a week and three days after our wedding, depriving her of both her son and her husband in a span of only 10 days. She tried so hard not to be intrusive in our early-married days, but with the arrivals of the children, she was always available to babysit, to come to the house to entertain them so I could accomplish one task or another, to can fruit with me, help me hang curtains or houseclean. She would miss us terribly, I knew. And the children and Bill and I would miss her.

The losses of my grandmother and mother had been terrible blows to me. Mom K quietly tried to fill those huge gaps in my life and I loved her dearly for it. The word "mother-in-law" had unhappy connotations for some of my friends, but I was grateful for the mother-in-law I won in the marriage lottery.

While Mom helped John with his breakfast, my father rang the doorbell. Dad and Mother had been married nearly 30 years when Mum died suddenly. Dad was so miserable alone, but by the time of our move, he was contentedly embarked on his second marriage. I was relieved to see my father so much happier.

Briskly stamping snow off his feet, Dad cheerfully asked what he could start to pack. I suggested he put the children's nightclothes and bedtime huggy-toys into the suitcases beside their beds, so he climbed the stairs to start that job. Mom asked what I would like her to do. I asked her to keep John comforted while I did last-minute kitchen chores.

Soon, the packers arrived, immediately bringing in a box for Oley's cage. We put him into it so he wouldn't be frightened by all the commotion. The men asked what to leave for us to take along and fanned out to pack all the rest. One of them went down to the fruit cellar beneath the kitchen to pack up — on my instructions — "everything on the shelves of home-canned fruit."

Mom K and I canned the fruit together. That might be the last of the home-canned fruit. I didn't know if I could ever face the huge job of canning by myself in our new home. When our goods were unpacked in New Jersey, we discovered that the packer had carefully included a 12-inch segment of the original ceiling beam from the fruit cellar. After we purchased the dishwasher and changed the alignment of appliances in our kitchen, the floor began to sag. When Bill replaced the old 12-inch-square, hand-hewn beam beneath it with a steel I-beam, he found it impossible to remove the old beam without cutting it into pieces. One of them must have been left on the shelf behind the canning jars. The worker followed instructions. He wrapped up "everything" on the shelves of home-canned fruit!

The packers finished quickly and the moving truck arrived. The outdoor swing set and sand box, the furniture and packed boxes were quickly stacked into the van, but, no matter what they did, they couldn't fit John's highchair inside. It had been Bill's first, then Gail's, David's and now John's. They lashed it to the back door of the van. It wasn't yet noon as I watched them drive away. The highchair was the last thing I saw as the truck turned the corner.

The house looked so empty and sad. Dad packed our suitcases in his car trunk, turned on the engine to warm up the car, then took Oley's box out to stow it safely. He placed Beth's carrier bed where Gail and David could sit on either side of it. Dad, Mom K, and the children climbed in, John immediately claiming Mom's lap. They waited while I walked through the house once more — no hint left there of our lives but the bright wallpaper, the tiled kitchen ceiling, the beautiful floors. There was nothing left on the windows but paper roll-up blinds, which I pulled down as I left each room. The house looked so dark and deserted! I comforted myself that new owners would soon fill it with life and laughter.

As I walked through the front door, I kissed my fingertips and touched them to the doorframe, whispering, "Goodbye, House. I hate to leave you. But you'll have nice new owners." I was eager to be with Bill again, so I locked it carefully and hid the key beneath the milk box on the porch, as prearranged with the buyers. None of the neighbors were outside that cold, gray day to wave goodbye.

MOVING ON

After lunch at Mom's, we put Oley's box back into the car, then said our goodbyes to Mom, who did her best not to let us see the tears in her eyes. At the airport, Dad turned over our luggage to a porter, parked the car, then — carrying Oley's box — checked at the desk to be sure our baggage was properly directed to our destination.

Carrying Beth's portable bed, holding Johnny's hand and trying to herd Gail and David through the crowded terminal was a challenge. The older two tended to see something interesting and wander off to investigate. It would have been easy to lose them there. But we safely met Dad at the airlines desk.

Dad helped me to the gate with the children. That was long before airline security; Dad was my security. I could not have done it without him. In addition to the children, I had a small bag of toys to keep the children entertained on the flight, a diaper bag, a half dozen bottles of Beth's formula in an insulated bag, Mrs. White's package of baked goods — plus Oley in his box.

Dad helped entertain the children while we waited to board the airplane, until the official at the desk told Dad he could help me board early. He did, stowing Oley, Beth's carrier bed, and all the rest of our hand luggage. After seeing us settled in our seats, Dad hugged and kissed the children, then me. Married at not-quite-20, I had never traveled out of town except for our honeymoon. Now, at 27, I was moving away for good. My eyes were misty as I watched my father exit the plane.

Gail and David bounced in their seats with excitement, watching the bustle of activity outside the windows. David sat at the window, Gail beside him, with Beth's carrier bed next to her in the aisle seat directly across from mine. Knowing that Johnny, not quite 18 months of age, would be frightened by all the commotion, I seated him beside me. The empty window seat on my side held Oley's box.

We could feel the rumble of engines while the plane climbed. Once altitude was reached, the engines slowed to cruising speed, the strong vibrations changing to a low hum. "Mommy, why are we stopping?" David asked loudly. Nearby passengers chuckled as I assured him we hadn't stopped, but were now cruising at the correct altitude so the engines no longer needed to work so hard to climb higher in the sky. Noting the changing scene beneath our plane, David was relieved to agree that we were indeed still moving.

Beth slept well till the middle of the short flight. When she awakened, the stewardess heated her bottle quickly, then offered to take John for a walk down the aisle. But he hid his face and clung to me until Gail offered to sit beside him. The stewardess moved Oley's box to the seat Gail vacated so she could sit in the window seat to hold John's hand while I fed and changed Beth. As soon as I finished, Beth went right back to sleep, lulled by the hum of the engines. When I sat down again, John climbed back into my lap, popped his fingers into his mouth and buried his face in my shirt. Relieved of the duty of comforting her little brother, Gail sat quietly looking out the window.

Our arrival was smooth. Touchdown was barely noticeable, but John cried frantically because his ears hurt. I tried to give him chewing gum, but he would have none of it. I told him to swallow so his ears would feel better, but he was crying too hard to hear me. We taxied to a stop. "We're here, Johnny! Daddy will be coming for us. Watch for Daddy! Daddy will be here soon!" John's ears must have "popped" then. Suddenly relieved of pain, his sobbing subsided. Gail and David stood in their seats watching the flurry of activity inside the plane.

The aircraft soon emptied. David yelled, "Da-a-ah-DEEEEE!" Climbing past Oley's box and Beth's carrier, he raced down the aisle to launch himself at Bill. Gail clambered past Oley's box, John and me but, as befitted the eldest, she walked sedately down the aisle to say, "Daddy, I'm glad to see you." Bill shook her hand formally and bent over to kiss her with David in one arm. Standing, he caught my eye and grinned. As soon as he could reach me, he wrapped his other arm around John and me, kissed me warmly, closed his eyes and whispered in my ear, "You're *here*. You're really <u>here</u>." Opening his eyes again, he told me, "I missed you *so much!*"

Bill managed all our carry-on luggage at once — either in his hands or tucked under his arms. David bounced along in front of him. Gail carried Oley's box. I held the handle of Beth's carrier and John's hand. Just then, the pilot exited the cabin. Looking past Bill to the rest of us, he said, "Wow! You have *your* hands full, Buddy!" "Men!" I grumped to myself. "What does he think *I* do in this partnership? — WE have *our* hands full, Mister; thank you very much!" Having always been somewhat feisty, my reaction was a little ahead of the coming women's movement.

We headed up the ramp to the terminal. John became tearful again — too much change, too many people milling around, too much newness for him to comprehend. Bill found a porter who loaded Oley and the carry-on luggage onto his cart. Taking Beth's carrier from me, Bill led us through the terminal to the baggage claim area where he placed the carrier on a seat near the window. He asked Gail to please sit beside Beth to look after her while we claimed our bags. David decided to sit on the other side of Beth to "help Gail." Assuring them we wouldn't be out of their sight, Bill and I went to pluck our bags off the carousel, turned them over to the porter, then Bill picked up Beth's carrier again. With John still clinging to me tightly, we all followed Bill to our car in the parking structure. Once the luggage, Oley and the other children were settled in, I sank into the front seat with John on my lap. The rest of the day would be easier. We were all together again.

Gail and David were excited about the hotel room. They turned on faucets in the bathroom, fingered the sample toothpaste and shampoo. Unwrapping two mini-bars of soap, they washed their hands just to see how everything worked. John, in my arms, eyes like saucers, looked around warily. Bill put Beth's carrier in a corner so nobody could trip over it. She continued sleeping soundly.

Removing Oley's cage from the box, Bill put fresh water into the container, emptied into his dish a small bag of seed I had taped to the outside of the cage, then latched the door again. Oley must have been mystified! He had last been in his familiar corner in our dining room, then was closed up in the dark for hours feeling his cage moved and the vibrations of automobile and airplane engines. Now here he was in a totally strange place!

I handed Johnny to Bill and stretched out on the bed. It felt so good! I thought I could sleep for a week! But just then, John surprised us by announcing, "I hungry!" The rest of us enjoyed Mrs. White's baked goods on the plane, but Johnny would have none of them. Gail and David decided they were hungry, too. "Should we call room service or go to the restaurant?" Bill asked me. I decided we needed to become acquainted with the restaurant then and there, with Bill to help. But it wasn't half as hectic as I expected. The children were well behaved, John surprised us by eating well, and Beth slept through it all.

Back in our room, Bill reached into the closet for a big bag he left there before meeting us. It was filled with new toys, coloring books and crayons. While Gail and David explored the new treasures, John found a stuffed bunny he liked and climbed back onto my lap to cuddle it.

Suddenly Beth erupted, hungry and demanding. For such a tiny baby, she certainly had a loud voice! I handed John to Bill and dealt with Beth. When Beth was back in her carrier, John surprised us by falling asleep in Bill's arms. I undressed him, waking him in the process. Warily, I put him into the hotel crib, expecting tears. Instead, he settled down sleepily, satisfied to hold my hand for the moment it took him to fall sound asleep again. It must have been an even more tiring day of worry for him than I realized! Gail and David were heavy-eyed, too, and eagerly hopped into the two roll-out beds Bill unfolded for them. Bill and I considered watching TV, but I was tired, too.

How unimaginably comforting it was to just snuggle "spoon-fashion" with Bill! I was "home" again even if everything was new and different. The next few days in the hotel might present challenges, but I fell asleep in two blinks. We were all together again; a completely new life awaited us all.

THE DISASTER HOUSE

After only two days in the hotel, we moved into what we called "the disaster house."

I had not seen it before we met the movers there, which was merciful. As in Buffalo, housing was scarce with so many returning veterans rapidly raising the nation's population totals. Seeking a landlord who would rent without a lease to a family with four small children made the search extremely challenging for Bill, who had to settle for whatever he could find available.

As I stepped out of the car, I saw an old Victorian house so tall it's mansard roof appeared to touch the low, gray clouds, it's paint faded to a sickly yellow with once-scarlet trim then almost pink. Un-curtained windows stared like blind eyes. Situated on a main highway, cars sped past at 50 mph. Just then, a train came roaring along the Jersey Central main railway line — directly across the road! We couldn't even hear John's terrified shrieks until the train passed. When I took him from the car, he clung to me for dear life, shuddering with panicky sobs.

When we entered, my eyes were drawn up … and up … and UP! Directly in front of me a stairway looked like Jacob's ladder to heaven. My heart sank at the thought of carting Johnny up those stairs! I handed him to Bill so I could explore; I needed to tell the movers where to put the furniture.

Nothing about that house was comfortable or convenient! The kitchen was miniscule, the living room so tiny we used it only to store temporarily unused furniture. The dining room had to serve as playroom/family room, and the back door led to a small, square open landing and rickety steps to a back yard with *no* fencing.

There were four doors and three archways leading from the kitchen. The four doors led to the backyard, the basement (which I didn't take time to explore), to the steepest, most narrow stairway I had ever seen (the back stairs the hired girl once used), and to a small, cramped bathroom. There were also archways providing passage to the dining room and front hall. Table, chairs, and high chair would barely fit in the skimpy floor space in front of the double window. A stove with no counters on either side, a sink and drainboard with cabinets beneath and above provided no work counter at all.

I started up the lengthy front stairway. Bill, still holding John, watched me with a worried frown. There were three bedrooms — two at the back of the house, one at the front, and an enormous bathroom (which had probably been a bedroom in the days before indoor plumbing).

Girls in one, boys in the other? That would put Beth in the same room with Gail, who had to wake for school. No way! OK, how about Beth in our room, two boys in the small back bedroom so John could see us across the hall and Gail by herself in the front room? That's how I told the movers to distribute the furniture. It didn't work. John never settled down happily day or night in that house, so that very first night, we transferred David into Gail's room.

The first morning there, David awakened with one ear so swollen from some sort of bite that it doubled over. Bedbugs? Fleas? Spiders? Whatever could be in that room to bite him? But Gail had no bites; it was a mystery. It turned out that three-quarters of the yet-unseen basement was ankle-deep in water and hosted a thriving population of mosquitoes hatching near the furnace. In midwinter! David was allergic to mosquito bites. With antihistamine pills to help David, mosquito repellent for all of us, and insect spray in the basement, we finally conquered that problem. But water in the basement endangered our washer and dryer the movers had installed without thought to the flood. We disconnected them, raised them on blocks and I traipsed to the laundromat a couple of times a week as long as we lived there! Even with Gail in kindergarten, it was difficult enough with only the other three children to wait for the wash to finish. Drying laundry there was prohibitively time-consuming during Gail's half-day school hours. The flood in the basement never drained away; it just rose and fell a bit, so I had to hang clothes outdoors no matter what the weather.

No fence around the back yard, a 50-mph highway in front and the Jersey Central Main Line directly across the road! John, who could run like the wind, could not possibly be outdoors without my entire attention. Nor could I leave him indoors while I hung out laundry. Bill explored the hardware store and found a harness and pulley to hang on the laundry line. It was made for a dog run, but it might save the day. I altered the harness to fit Johnny, we tethered him to the line and Bill hung a parallel line for the wash. John loved action! He shrieked with excited laughter running that line every time I hung out laundry or watched the older children playing in the yard — unless a train passed, at which he always dissolved into terrified tears!

If I happened to be on the phone when a train passed, I learned to shout into it that I would call back in a few minutes — and simply hang up. I couldn't hear any response to my announcement so I had to leave it to chance. When I did call back, the inevitable questions arose, "*What* was that *terrible* noise? What *happened* there?"

An endless stairway, an almost-useless back yard (which still had to be mowed in the summer!), a perpetually wet basement, no laundry facilities, no air conditioning, no playmates for the children, traffic noises, the house-rattling train — that was the "disaster house."

AND STILL MORE DISASTERS!

That house not only WAS a disaster; it seemed to be a focus for other disasters.

At three months of age, Beth began to shriek in pain. A midnight trip to the emergency room — with ALL the children! — revealed the reason. She had a hernia and a strangulated intestine. The doctor pushed the intestine back in, taped the hernia, sent us home, told us she was young enough for it to heal over. He was wrong. It happened again, then still again on the opposite side — disasters seemed at home in that house! Beth finally had surgery to correct paired hernias, a birth defect caused by her prematurity.

Then one night when Bill was on a training trip to Headquarters in Houston, and all the children were sleeping, the house was invaded! I was quietly writing letters home when I heard a noise … a thud … then footsteps on the basement stairs. Dropping my pen, I turned the television on LOUD so the intruder would know someone was home, and ran to be sure the basement door was locked. Racing back to the dining room, I dialed the police, told them I was home alone with four young children and heard an intruder in the basement. They promised to be there in minutes, but it may have been *seconds;* they had experienced similar calls previously. Four police cruisers drove right up over the curb to the front of the house itself. Policemen erupted from cars and seemed to run in every direction. The largest patrolman I had ever seen ran up the front steps to the door I was already opening. "Where is he?" he huffed. "In the basement," I replied, gesturing down the hallway. Passing me, he unlocked the basement door, flung it open, turned on his flashlight and ran down the stairs.

The basement window had been removed but no intruder was found. Muddy tracks were left on the floor beneath the opening. Hearing the TV, the intruder must have fled immediately. The officers nailed the window back in place and told me they would put the house on their "watch list," promising to drive by several times a day and night. I wasn't entirely reassured, but there seemed nothing further could be done. One night seven months later, a teenager was caught on his way out of a local auto dealership, with a notebook in his pocket listing all the houses and businesses he had entered, including ours — "for the thrill of outsmarting the police!"

THE NEW HOUSE

In the meantime, we found a new subdivision and a house plan we liked. It was to be built on a soon-to-be-paved street in Westfield, an upscale community with the reputation of good schools. With Bill's G.I. mortgage available to us by transfer, the profit and equity from the house in Cold Spring provided our down payment. The salesman mentioned that both the street and the house foundation had already been staked and roped. So one nice Sunday afternoon in early spring, we decided to view our new lot.

Driving off the pavement onto the staked-out roadway, heading toward the other end of the sub, Bill realized our wheels were sinking ever deeper as we drove. Speeding up, he hoped to reach the paving in the slightly older neighborhood at the end of the new sub. Accustomed to Buffalo's winter ground deeply frozen till late Spring, we were unprepared for New Jersey's softer mud layer beneath a thin frozen skin. Despite Bill's efforts, we mired down exactly in front of our staked foundation, two building lots from the pavement at the other end, too deep in muck for him to open the door.

Bill climbed out the window, carried the children piggyback, one by one, to the pavement, his shoes and slacks becoming heavier with mud on each trip. Gail minded David first, then John. When Beth was placed in Gail's arms, David forcibly held John by the back of his collar oblivious to his howls of rage while Bill returned for me.

When Bill knocked on the door of the nearest house to ask to use their phone to call a tow truck, the housewife was horrified. "NO," she said, "you're too muddy! I'll do it for you."

The truck arrived but the driver refused to wade through the mud, so Bill slogged back again to attach a tow-chain to our car. The truck's engine strained and roared multiple times without moving the car an inch. Finally, the driver offered to drive us home and return in the morning with a larger truck — and a power winch. Bill left his ruined shoes and slacks on the back porch and hurried indoors wrapped in the towel I handed him.

In mid-afternoon the next day, a vehicle-sized blob of mud was deposited in our driveway. The winch succeeded in pulling our car out of the muck, along with a goodly portion of NJ real estate. When Bill came home from work, he found our garden hose, hooked it up, and began hosing off the car. A river of mud ran into the highway but in an hour, Bill managed to wash off only enough mud to clear the windshield and open the door. He drove to an automatic car wash, where it took several trips through the power-wash before he recognized our vehicle. We waited till the road to our new house was paved before attempting a repeat visit to our home-to-be.

Just before Thanksgiving, we moved into our brand-new, modern, split-level house and transferred Gail to Westfield schools. The following Spring, the developer planted shrubs and grass seed. The house had a large back yard with a five-acre park behind it, was second from the end of the newly-paved street barriered at the town line to make it a dead-end with almost no traffic. Living room, dining room, kitchen, family room, a *dry* basement laundry, four bedrooms with room for a fifth above the living room (which Bill soon finished for the boys to share), a safe neighborhood full of playmates for the children, and highly rated schools! — that house served us well for the next 11 years. Bill joined a carpool to work so I could carpool kids to school.

Bill's mom moved from Buffalo to a small house a short way from ours. We and the children were so glad to have their grandmother near again! When promotions later sent Bill into New York City to work, the town was situated conveniently astride the Jersey Central railroad, providing an easy commute. He passed the "disaster house" daily during those trips.

ANNE MARGARET

In the Westfield house, we had our last baby, Anne Margaret, who arrived the morning of January first, 1964 — in the middle of a snowstorm. We barely made it to the hospital in time!

The baby's ETA was December 21st. I worried about missing Christmas with the children. But that holiday passed safely and soon it was time for a neighborhood New Year's Eve party. Our hosts prepared a special chair just for me — enveloped in towels with a water-filled bucket beside it containing a huge pair of tinsnips!

We left the party about 2:00 a.m. Walking across the street to our house, we noted that the stars we saw earlier were hidden by clouds. At 6:00 a.m., I awakened to strong contractions and roused Bill who dressed quickly and went to warm the car. I shook Gail awake — she was then 14 — to tell her she was in charge 'til she could call her grandmother to come take over.

Bill, snow on his hair and boots, called from the foot of the bedroom stairs. "We have a problem," he said. "Hurry! There's a major snowstorm going on! We'll have trouble getting up the hill to Overlook hospital!"

We did run into heavy snow and slippery roads. My labor was becoming very insistent along with the storm. Bill finally said, "I know we're close to the hospital, but I can't see where we're going. I'm afraid I'll drive us off the road. You'll have to drive while I walk ahead of the car to guide you." Contractions notwithstanding, I slid into the driver's seat and drove with my head out the window watching Bill wading through snow ahead of the car until we saw the hospital's lights. Anne was born within 15 minutes of our arrival. It *was* a close call!

Anne enjoyed six "parents" since her siblings all vied to help care for her. She had to be the most secure baby in ten counties! When Anne was an infant, Gail and David often argued over whose turn it was to change her! When their battles waxed too fierce, I handed each of them a bottle of Windex, ordering them to polish opposite sides of the French door leading to the patio while *I* changed Anne. In no time, they were laughing at each other's fierce scowls seen through the glass.

THOSE BUSY WESTFIELD YEARS

— in our fifth home, were good years. Bill completed school and became *Doctor* Keeber, our family grew and thrived. Bill was handy at repairs or renovations and I learned to keep house efficiently while also caring for five growing children. In Westfield, I carpooled, and carpooled … and carpooled! And sometimes wondered which was my primary residence — the house or the station wagon.

Bill had a quick, wry sense of humor most often directed at himself. Modestly, he refused to use his hard-earned academic title except professionally, and only then when he felt it best for business. But one day, a bumptious, self-important newcomer to the company Medical department pushed his buttons too far. He called the lab, barking imperiously into the phone, "Hello! Is Keeber there? This is Doctor Smith!" "Why, yes, Smith," Bill replied, "this is <u>Doctor</u> Keeber. What may I do for you?"

Thrift was important. A new house and four growing children still stretched Bill's excellent salary. I added knitting and sewing to my list of new skills and kept the children well supplied with scarves, sewed most of the girls' school dresses, Gail's dance and prom gowns. Gail learned to sew, too, making several outfits for herself and her sisters. With the help of the sewing machine, I thriftily clothed myself as fashionably as I could, since — by that time — Bill had moved into sales and his job included entertaining. I loved that, because I was able to dine out with him, his clients and their wives — and meet so many interesting people. Grandma was always happy to stay with the family, even when industry conventions took me to Atlantic City for several days as Bill's "official" hostess, a luxurious hotel interlude for me.

We lived in Westfield until John was ready to start middle school. The school system push-push-pushed for high achievement so as many students as possible could be accepted at Ivy League colleges. By that time, we believed the children would do better with less pressure, so we moved to a smaller town.

MIDDLESEX

Our new address would be Middlesex, NJ. We expected to move in the summer, but by August, the houses had not even been started because of a deed-glitch. There were none at all available for rent in the school district. Our Westfield house was to be occupied by the new owners in late August.

With the start of the school year looming, I located all the houses listed for sale, called at each one — offering to rent the house, to always have it ready to show when realtors brought through prospective buyers and to do my best to sell the house. No takers! — until I finally found one woman whose husband had already moved out of state. They, too, wanted their son to start school at their new location. We moved into that house just days before school began. I showed it successfully, so by the time our home was ready for occupancy the following January, new buyers were ready to move into our temporary home. My unorthodox idea worked successfully for all three families — sellers, renters and buyers.

Until Springtime, we entered our new house via a wooden walkway. New Jersey's soft winter mud prevented the pouring of sidewalks till then. But finally, they were in and we began landscaping. That property had once been a nursery ground, so the soil was amazingly fertile. I enthused to Bill that I only had to walk outdoors with seeds in my hand for the earth to reach up and grab them! I quickly lost my

World War II Victory Garden aversion to weeding. It was a joy to garden there since nothing planted failed to thrive!

Middlesex was known as the "greenhouse capital" of New Jersey, with a larger concentration of greenhouses in that small town than any other place in the state. Also fascinated by the ease of growing things, Beth couldn't stay away from greenhouses she passed on her way home from middle school. One owner, a grandmotherly lady, took Beth under her wing and taught her a great deal about flowers. If Beth didn't show up at home right after school, I knew she'd be home just after 5:00 p.m. when the greenhouse closed. Beth's love of flowers was firmly rooted in those years.

During our three-and-a-half years in Middlesex, Gail volunteered as a Candy Striper, graduated from high school and trained to become a Practical Nurse. Later, she continued her education to become a Registered Nurse. David graduated from Middlesex High School, too, and John completed middle school, with Beth just a year behind him.

We all enjoyed hosting a college exchange student one summer there. The children took him to their hearts as an older brother. Josef was from Austria, an only child who never knew the father lost in his infancy. Family life was a happy revelation to him. That summer he watched historic events on television with Bill, Gail and David — including the horrifying assassination of Robert Kennedy. They talked politics, ethics, science, and life in general. Josef became a life-long friend, one with whom we corresponded over the years and visited twice at his home in Austria. He became an important part of our extended family, despite his short residence with us. When we had to write to Josef about Bill's death many years later, Josef wrote that he, too, mourned the only father he had known, who strongly influenced his own life, and from whom he said he learned to be a father. Bill was a mentor to many in his life, mostly at work, but Josef was also a beneficiary of his interest in seeing others grow into their potential.

Bill's job changed from the sales to the marketing division, which he found an even more interesting challenge. After three-and-a-half years in Middlesex, Bill was transferred to Michigan for another promotion. So once again, we prepared to move, and Mom agreed to move, too.

DISCIPLINE FOR DUMMIES!

That was the course title for my on-the-job-training over the growing-up years for our family. I was raised with my grandmother's admonitions that "If you give them an inch, they'll surely take a mile." The daughter of a ship captain, she believed, "It's a poor captain who can't keep his crew under control."

In my early parenting years, Bill was at college, studying or working. After he began to tread his career path, Bill's primary day job was to support us, while mine was to run the household and care for the children. Bill dealt with discipline when he was at home, but I was the one down there in the trenches, in the thick of the action — present at the moment most discipline was required. Thus, from the beginning, I became the primary disciplinarian by default.

Parents-to-be seem to come in two styles. Some, dissatisfied with their own experiences on the receiving end of parental discipline, are convinced they will never speak harshly nor spank their future offspring. Others firmly espouse the "spare the rod, spoil the child" theory, and plan on allowing no leeway. Both types seem equally confused when first facing their own fractious children.

I developed (á la my grandma) what our children still refer to as "the evil eye." When they misbehaved, I aimed at them what I called "the look." I thought it had a positive effect. They say it was a paralyzing effect.

Whatever. It worked. Some of the time. I also (á la Grandma) tended to use "time outs" in solitary bedrooms or in corners as a disciplinary tool.

That being, however, the tail end of the "spare the rod, spoil the child" era, parents who did not occasionally resort to spanking were considered poorly equipped for the job. Regardless of their built-in opinions on discipline, many parents — faced with the thought of physically striking that being who, until that moment, had been the apple of his or her eye — were torn with either indecision or guilt. I was among that throng, often too quick to act, but long to feel guilt.

Gail was mischievous, always ready to push the limits of my patience. David was even more mischievous, but so creative about it! Each of the first four, in turn, earned that designation in his or her individual way. None of them ever did anything really bad, nor anything intentionally mean or unkind. But they often closely skirted the edge of unacceptable.

Anne, born nine years after the fourth, was a different story — an extremely biddable child. She had six doting "parents," her own two and four older siblings. She barely had the opportunity to misbehave since all the family watched over her so unremittingly. But when she did, a woeful expression and "Anne, I am *so* disappointed in you," were all it took to return her to equilibrium. Oddly enough, she has grown up to be a strongly opinionated adult who takes no static from anyone. She manages to say the most frankly honest things to people like bosses or coworkers without giving offense. A loving mom, she is still a strict disciplinarian with her own daughter. Go figure! I'm told the apple falls not far from the tree, but I only *wish* I had the ability to speak my mind as easily and non-aggressively as Anne! And to exert control on her child with as little negative reaction as Anne experiences!

One of my methods of discipline was intimidation. I threatened a spanking after waiting a reasonable time for bad behavior to stop. Then I counted, "One —two — two and uh … h-h ha-a-alf … … twooo-aaand-threee-quaaarter-r-r-r-rs (hoping I would not have to follow through!) — <u>THREE</u>!" On that cue, I marched menacingly toward the miscreants, who almost always retreated, yelling as if they'd already been spanked.

Warnings and intimidation notwithstanding, they occasionally pushed the limits beyond my endurance. Sometimes, I grabbed the yardstick, raised it high in the air, whizzed it rapidly and audibly downwards, stopped just before it touched a bottom or a leg, then tapped the offender. The result was usually just as effective as a sound spanking. Convinced they had been half-killed, they roared with dismay, cried great huge tears of "pain," and then behaved.

When Gail was a pre-schooler, she was insistently naughty all one morning. As I whizzed the yardstick rapidly downward from a great height, it struck the chrome leg of our enameled kitchen table. The yardstick snapped, the broken piece flew across the room, bounced off the wall and clattered to the floor. Gail, hearing the whizz, then the snap, grabbed at her backside, jumped up and down, screamed blue murder and produced huge tears. When I burst out laughing, she was entirely mystified. I think she still firmly believes I broke the yardstick on her derriere!

As the children grew, I found another method successful. They loved those little paddles from the Five & Dime store with a ball attached to each by a long elastic band. When the bands broke, I claimed the trashed paddles, wrote names on each and tucked them into a kitchen drawer. If behavior became unacceptable despite warnings, I told the miscreant, "Alright! Go get *your* paddle!" As adults, they maintain that the ensuing paddlings, which I kept reasonably mild — but you'd never believe *that* from t*heir* accounts! — were nowhere near as bad as the agony of having to find "their own" paddles, bring them to me, and "back up" to the music!

When that darling infant with the sweet smile first metamorphoses into a little demon who will *not* follow directions, it's a terrible shock to every parent! This matter of discipline is always touchy. As Grandma said, "No captain who loses control of his crew can easily regain their respect." But how to maintain that control is often a mystery to parents, new and seasoned ones alike. No "one size fits all." Some children can best be controlled, as was Anne, with a sad look and "I'm *so* disappointed in you." Others, like David, seem to persistently campaign for the "woodshed" treatment (or a convincing facsimile) no matter how hard the parent tries to escape that.

To avoid the need for disciplinary action, parents do, over time, develop a "second sense" when it comes to detecting skullduggery in process. Evidences to me of trouble to be stopped in its tracks were silences in the children's normally noisy play or whispered conferences between them. I warned the children that mothers are given eyes in the backs of their heads and can also see around corners. It was not until Gail crept behind my easy chair when I was reading, and gently parted my hair with her fingers to find no concealed eyes that my warnings began to be suspected.

Some incidents I recall illustrate a few of the problems faced by parents — and sometimes children.

David was especially creative with his mischief. My greatest problem with him was that he amused me so much with his originality that it was difficult to be angry with him over things I would not accept from his siblings. In fairness, I had to try and sometimes over-reacted.

David didn't always get away scot-free, despite his talent at judging the depth of my impatience nearly to a T. He often pushed the limits a little at a time, counting on my cooling down between irritations. When he misjudged once, as he gleefully reminded me some 50 years after the incident, I spanked him.

His indignant response was a heartfelt, "I hate you!" That was one step too far. I roared at him, "You do NOT! I'm your mother; you *love* me!" Far from repentant, he repeated, "NO! I hate you!" Smack! "I hate you!" Smack! "I still hate you!" I can't recall how long it took him to realize that discretion was the better part of valor, but he did capitulate. "I love you, Mommy (sob, sob!)" I can't say that was a "Mommy Dearest" memory I was thrilled to recall, but it's part of the story, too. Parents are not saints; they occasionally take actions at odds with their theories when emotion clouds their thinking.

Beth was eight when we announced to the children that a new sibling was on the way. "Well, it's about time!" she declared. "I'm sick and tired of being the baby around here!" She requested that the infant be assigned her room across the hall from Bill's and mine so she could move to the unoccupied bedroom on the ground level of our quad-level house, which her three older siblings thought too solitary for comfort.

The only problem there was that Beth seemed to be "in trouble" so much of the time! My usual punishment was to confine her to her room — until I noticed her playing in the back yard when I thought she was "in solitary confinement." I began locking Beth into her room for her specified "times out." Nevertheless, when an unexpected downpour drove the children indoors, Beth, locked in her room just minutes before the rain, ran into the house along with her siblings. She had taken to climbing out her ground-floor window, returning just in time for me to "free" her after the "sentence" was completed. But the rain deep-sixed her timing!

Beth and John were usually happy playmates and companions. But Beth, the family's most adventurous climber, was once smartly smacked on her bottom after coming to tell me I needed to help John, who was yelling for help to get down out of a tree. "You KNOW he hates heights!" I told her, immediately envisioning what happened. "Only *you* could have taunted him into climbing up there — and then you *deserted* him!"

Did I make mistakes? Of course I did. I spanked too often, over-guilted my children, and praised them too little. Do I wish I could "do over" some things? Certainly — but that's not a choice. My children and I have to live with the effects and fallout of my best, and sometimes worst, efforts. But I'm fortunate in having loving, caring (and forgiving) children. They don't blame me for kinks in their psyches. And I easily forgive them for driving me 'round the bend on more than one occasion for all the joy and laughter they gave me. Hate, forgiveness, acceptance, love — they're all part of the experience of a family.

Despite the difficulties and pitfalls inherent in being a disciplinarian, I ascribed to Grandma's theory that an undisciplined child is an insufficiently loved child. I was committed to her belief that a parent's most important job is to succeed, in whichever way works best for each individual child, in turning out a successful, moral, law-abiding adult. I was convinced it was up to me to teach my children right from wrong, and, on occasion, to enforce compliance. It seemed a daunting responsibility, but I accepted Grandma's dictum that without parents committed to effective discipline, children might grow into unhappy, unsuccessful adults. The question is always going to be — did I succeed? Or not? It may depend on the moment and the memory dredged up in that instant.

But the mystery remains. How best to achieve that end? It's always a trial-and-error exercise for each parent and each child. Probably nobody knows for sure how to discipline children, their own or others, since each family, each child, each incident is different. I know people who say with certitude, "If that were *my* child, I would never stand for that." If that were indeed the person's child, he or she would be a different child, and the problem would be a different problem.

    I always considered discipline a course for dummies — a permanent on-the-job training program, one from which Bill and I could never "graduate," but could never withdraw. Fortunately, we "timed out" when our children outgrew our efforts.

SENTIMENTAL JOURNEY HOME

When we planned a sentimental visit back to Cold Spring several years after our departure from Buffalo, it was bittersweet to find that our lovingly cared-for, life-warmed little house, and the Connaughy's and Mrs. Hureck's, had all been razed to make room for a new, brightly painted, subsidized low-income home. It was built on one generous, neatly-fenced lot, nicely landscaped with shrubs and flowers. A large vegetable bed grew just about where Mrs. Hureck's house once stood.

We visited Janine, a friend down the block with whom I maintained a correspondence over the years. In her always-cheerful letters, my friend told us only about her husband's promotions at work, her appointment to director of the nursing school at a nearby hospital, their son's marriage and children, their daughter's graduation from divinity school and call to serve as the pastor of a Cold Spring church. But Janine remained staunchly silent about the old neighborhood in our letters back and forth — until we visited. It was then that she finally told us about our old neighbors and the continued decline of the Cold Spring we had left.

Mrs. Fisher died peacefully soon after we left, with Mr. Fisher slipping quietly away in his sleep just weeks later. The Fishers belonged to the same Catholic Church as the Connaughys. There was no family, so the Connaughy boys volunteered to be pallbearers at both funerals.

Mrs. White and "Uncle" lived quietly on in their determinedly neat house — no matter what happened to the houses near theirs — for several years until their deaths. "Uncle" went first, then Mrs. White died about a year after him. Janine said that Mrs. White finally confessed to her that she and "Uncle" were illegal immigrants from the Caribbean who had escaped their poverty-stricken island to make a good life for themselves in Cold Spring. That was why they never told anyone their real names. When my friend asked for that information at the last, Mrs. White said it didn't matter since they had no children and there was nobody left "at home" who would know them anymore. She gave Janine the name of a lawyer contracted to make her final arrangements. So she was "Mrs. White" to the end.

Busy Mrs. Hureck died unexpectedly from a heart attack only about five years after we left. It occurred to me that if she had known her drafts from her retirement fund would be so few, she and Hal might have married, after all. But she never knew, so they did not. Janine said Hal was accepted at the county old folks' home, where he lived on comfortably for a few more years, occasionally visited by my friend.

The Connaughys left after the tenants in "our" house became too rowdy. Mrs. Connaughy told Janine that Mr. Connaughy was to retire soon. The older boys had already left home but the others refused to leave their parents alone there. Rather than delay their sons' plans for their own lives, she and Mr. Connaughy found a nice little house in the suburbs for their retirement. Janine couldn't remember to which town they had gone but she clearly recalled that all their boys were "as handsome as movie stars," and always so willing to be helpful.

"Hubby," his wife and family stayed on quietly, never speaking to any of the neighbors. Then one day, when the oldest boy neared high school age, they quietly moved out. The remaining neighbors thought of them as the "mystery family."

We asked about Moses. My friend paused, sighed, then said, "Poor Moses. He never really had a chance. His father took him into the 'family business'. He died on his 18th birthday in the front hall of his house right down the block in a shoot-out over a drug sale." She added, "But that house was torn down to make way for a nice, new one." We sat silently for a moment, remembering the strong, polite boy who played tea party with Gail and David, and smiled so delightedly as he handed toys to Johnny.

We finally asked about our old home. My friend told us that the sincere-sounding couple who admired the cheerful wallpaper, the shining wood floors and told us they couldn't wait to move in had never resided there at all. Instead they became absentee landlords, putting no money into upkeep as they rented to a long series of tenants. As the house became more and more ramshackle, they rented to multiple families to share it. The center porch post was broken one night in a drunken brawl. (That was when the Connaughys moved.) The porch roof sagged once more. The owners stopped paying taxes. The renters, no longer renting, became squatters. The house deteriorated even more quickly.

The Connaughy's and Mrs. Hureck's empty houses — rentals also abandoned by their owners — suffered the same fate as ours. After a series of police raids, the city reclaimed the properties for back taxes and evicted everyone. They stood vacant for a while except for occasional druggies who moved in for a night or two before the police arrested them. At last, all three houses were condemned and torn down. The attractive two-story house built in their place — with its fenced yard, neat shrubs, flowers and vegetable garden — was then home to a young family making good new memories of their own.

At the time of our visit, our block boasted several new subsidized low-income homes. The older houses still remaining were mostly painted and smart looking. Lawns flourished where none had been through all those years of ancient trees stealing all the nutrients from the soil. As the huge old trees died and were finally cut down, smaller decorative trees were planted here and there. The sun shone brightly on all the improvements. With streetlights no longer hidden in branches and leaves, the neighborhood was no longer dark at night, nor such a good harbor for lawbreakers.

Life there was much better than it had been at the end of our stay and afterwards — when Cold Spring went even farther downhill. I was glad for Janine, born, like Bill, in the old neighborhood. She doggedly stayed on through the old times, the bad times and the regeneration. Bill and I couldn't help feeling sentimental about the "old neighborhood" where Bill grew up and we lived our early married years. But that Cold Spring had become "history," just as the bad Cold Spring we left had done. Cold Spring then was a new and different place.

There were so many more good years for Bill and me following that time, but I'll never forget Al and Letty-Lou who sold us our fixer-upper house, its new kitchen ceiling accomplished with the shared labor of seller and buyers, its beautiful floors and pretty wallpaper. I'll always remember Mr. Snyder, the banker who banked on us on the strength of a handshake and walked away whistling when his confidence in us was proven well placed. It was there in that house, in pursuit of Bill's education and a better future for our family and ourselves, that we honed the ethic of hard work and responsibility. We were not aware then that, while we were learning to be strong partners, householders, and parents, we were also building the firm foundation for our many shared years. The Cold Spring of those years was where our good neighbors of such varied backgrounds taught us how, in our diversity and humanity, we shared values of caring and kindness.

That Cold Spring will always be alive and thriving – in my heart.

– AND <u>THEN</u> WHAT HAPPENED?

That was the question I asked my grandmother when she paused after telling me about my grandfather's death, her sale of all their belongings, the family's move to the United States. It was late and Grandma was tired of talking.

"The children grew up to become your mother and your aunts and your uncle," she replied abruptly. "And I became an old woman. — That's the end."

That wasn't really the end of the family story. It was only a pause for breath.

Over all those years since Grandma spoke, I grew up, Bill entered my life, our children grew up and, like my grandmother I, too, became an old woman. But the story does not end there, either. New beginnings were continually being made, all along the way.

There were our early "couple years," our "family years," then …

Gail, Bill's and my "responsible eldest," grew up to become a hospice nurse, a gentle soul, one of the peacemakers of the earth. Sentimental, loving, artistic and creative, she had two longed-for sons after 14 years of marriage. One of them is still pursuing his education, the other – graduated – is engaged to be married, a soon-to-be new beginning.

David struck out on his own, moving to Arizona in his early 20's, where he earned his MA to pursue a career he loved. He married twice, each marriage giving him a son. The eldest, now a college grad, has been seeing the world, trying on a variety of shoes for his walk into his future. The younger son is in college, pursuing an ambitious career-plan, envisioning golden new beginnings. Retired, David found new work with responsibilities and challenges and he continues to find more. He is a mover and shaker, adventurer, fisherman, athlete, fine woodworker, forever an instigator, thinker, people-person and he still makes me laugh.

John joined the Army. Missing home, he left at the end of his hitch, but joined the Reserves at home in Michigan, finally retiring from it after years of accumulated service. He worked at many jobs, culminating in the management of a motion picture sound studio with a sound-engineer partner much older than himself. The business closed when his partner's health failed. John, always a caregiver, looked after him till his death in 2011. Hampered by Michigan's unhealthy economy, John is still seeking his next new beginning.

Beth tried the world of health care, then branched out to more unusual jobs – machinist's helper, landscape worker, house painter. She moved to Florida, has two daughters and a son, whom she raised alone. Her daughters are both now in college, one balancing child care with her studies. Beth's son works hard in construction. Who knows where his path will lead him? Encountering difficulties along her way, Beth never achieved financial security, but she enjoys the good things in her life, "takes on" the less-than-good ones, savors her few blessings, is friendly, cheerful, courageous, as feisty as always and looking for new beginnings. The love of flowers she learned in Middlesex still intact, Beth enthusiastically e-mails pictures of her orchids to siblings. Beth is small but mighty, and, as ever, full of enthusiasm.

Anne, a certified paralegal in elder law practice, is extremely practical and capable, an avid gardener of mostly edibles, an enthusiastic vegetarian cook, busy with yoga and driving to and from her daughter's high school extra-curricular activities. Anne is busy, active, cheerful, a blue-eyed, red-haired force of nature. Her 16-year-old daughter demonstrates good values and positive attitudes, is "teen-enthusiastic" about new interests and friends. I can't wait to see where *her* path leads!

Bill traveled a great deal in his later career, in the US and overseas. As his work in marketing expanded, he traveled to Europe, South America, Asia, Australia. I often traveled overseas with him. We scheduled vacation time between and at the ends of his business endeavors. My youthful dreams of travel were fulfilled as we shared wonderful experiences all over the world — memories I now savor like gold coins trickling through my fingers just as did my grandmother with her memories of life with her two true loves.

As Bill neared retirement, he handed me a bankbook, saying, "I promised you this a long time ago. It took a while till we reached a point where it would be possible for you to take advantage of it, but this is your tuition for your long-postponed college degree." I joked over the years that while Bill earned his Ph.D., I earned my Ph.T. (Putting Hubby Through). Bill's own prodigious work and study-skills were certainly what took him through college and a successful career, but the jokes had their genesis in fact. He might not have continued on to his Ph.D., nor the corner office he finally occupied, without my partnership in our daily life, had I not been ready to cope independently at home. I grew so much in my own career as wife and mother and found so much satisfaction in the job that I no longer needed a parchment to prove myself nor prepare for a different career. I didn't care to spend any of Bill's retirement in a college classroom when I could spend it with him instead. I preferred to savor our couple years again after all our family years with the children we both wanted. Bill thought about what I said, then put his arms around me and told me, "I love you so much."

After Bill retired, he spent a few days watching my activities at home — then he said, "I don't have a single thing I absolutely *must* do each day, while you do necessary things every day for our comfort and health." With his scientist's analytical approach, he told me, "We need to go over exactly what you do, so we can divide up jobs according to our skills. That way, we'll each have equal time off after the necessities of our life are dealt with."

Bill took over some chores, leaving me free to do the others. If I worked longer in a day that he did he asked, "What part of that can I do?" Bill determinedly worked it out so we could enjoy "equal time off." We shared each other's activities but also gave one another time to pursue our individual passions, which we then shared in conversations over the dinner table. We thoroughly enjoyed what Bill always referred to as "our" retirement — enjoyed even-steven. Bill was such an egalitarian man!

When our children were growing, our vacations were mobile, educational ones, where we tried to show them the larger world beyond their own familiar horizons of home and neighborhood. Bill — always logical, practical — liked to plan daily travels directly, efficiently from Point A to Point B. I preferred to explore byways and surprises. The children still speak of "hysterical markers" when I saw signs indicating an Historical Marker ahead and shrieked excitedly for Bill to stop for me to read it aloud to the family! In those years, we traveled, first with a succession of smaller to larger tents, then camping and travel trailers.

After Bill's and my travels overseas during his career years, we enjoyed traveling in the United States after his retirement with a small, well-equipped travel trailer we lived in comfortably for a couple of months at a time. We savored the intimacy of the close space where we hugged doing dishes whenever we collided and cuddled in our almost-double bed. We made many more good memories in those years.

Bill and I were married for 59-and-a-half years. We worked together, we occasionally fought (mostly when I was going through menopause!), we loved each other, we hung in there, we took care of each other.

We lived in Buffalo for 7 years, then New Jersey for nearly 15, all good years. Then Bill was transferred to Michigan where he centered 'til he retired. Bill's mother moved from Buffalo to New Jersey to be near us, then again to Michigan. She lived to be 93, loved and treasured by all her family.

The last four of Bill's mostly contented and busy 20-year retirement were plagued with what turned out to be Parkinson's Disease. That further compromised the cumulative effects of nerve damage to those frozen feet so many years before. It was then that I helped Bill with things he could not do. I buttoned his shirts, put on his socks and shoes, steadied him when his walker became difficult for him, pushed his wheelchair when that became necessary. Bill never failed to thank me when I did something for him, nor — as added help became necessary — his home health aides. He was a gentleman and a gentle man. When speech became difficult for him, the one thing he most determinedly struggled to say was, "Me, too — you!" in response to my "I love you, Darling."

I was so lucky to have Bill's love for so many years. I wanted it to go on forever — our marriage vow to love, honor and cherish. But that contract was rendered null and void when Bill's death at 82 years of age activated that terminating clause our hearts never comprehended in our youth: "'til death us do part." I haven't stopped loving him, but I am no longer half of a pair pledged to one another in this life. I am now an individual who must stand on my own feet. I didn't make that choice, nor did Bill. It was just how it happened.

Widowed since 2007, I will always miss my very best friend and dearest love, but I have picked up the threads of my life, am finding so much good in life seeking new challenges, new friends, new activities, even new travel. Although in the age category where George Burns said he never bought green bananas, I plan to enjoy every day, week, month, year granted me with all the enthusiasm I can muster. I hope to begin my next chapter winded from the exertion but raring to go, always seeking new experiences, new adventures to, hopefully, share again with Bill someday.

While I have wonderful memories of all those years Bill and I had together, the years in Cold Spring were so special to me — the beginning of our long love story. But the story goes on. Each member of our family is building stories to someday tell their own children, nieces and nephews. There is no end — only multiple new beginnings.

I have reached the end of this tale, but more is being lived every day, so watch for the next installment …

TO BE CONTINUED

by ???